SBA Mortgage Loan Requirements, Rates, and Loan Structures

How to Compare SBA Mortgage Options, Understand Rates, and Choose the Best Loan

By Joseph G. Correa

Licensed Mortgage Broker, Finibi Mortgage

Copyright & Legal Notice

Published by Live Stronger Faster

The information provided in this book is for educational and informational purposes only and does not constitute financial, legal, tax, or investment advice. Although the author is a licensed mortgage professional, the content presented is general in nature and is not intended as personalized guidance for any specific individual, business, or financial situation.

The strategies, loan structures, and examples discussed in this book are illustrative and educational in nature. They are intended to demonstrate concepts related to SBA commercial mortgage financing, including SBA 7(a) and 504 loan programs, borrower qualification, debt service coverage analysis, property acquisition, refinancing, construction financing, and advanced loan structuring. These examples do not represent guaranteed approvals, loan terms, or outcomes. Results may vary significantly based on individual financial profiles, credit history, business performance, property type, market conditions, and lender-specific guidelines.

SBA loan programs are subject to eligibility requirements, regulatory guidelines, and changes established by the U.S. Small Business Administration and participating lenders. Borrowers are encouraged to consult directly with qualified financial, legal, and tax professionals before making any financing or investment decisions.

The author and publisher make no representations or warranties regarding the accuracy, completeness, or applicability of the content and disclaim any liability for errors, omissions, or outcomes resulting from the use or misuse of the information contained in this book.

All trademarks, service marks, company names, and product names referenced in this publication are the property of their respective owners and are used strictly for identification and educational purposes only. Their inclusion does not imply endorsement or affiliation.

First Edition, 2026

Table of Contents

Introduction

Understanding SBA mortgage loan requirements, interest rates, and loan structures is the turning point between simply qualifying for financing and mastering how to use financing as a strategic tool to build wealth, scale a business, and control real estate. Many borrowers approach SBA loans with a narrow focus: "Can I get approved?" But seasoned investors, business owners, and financially intelligent borrowers ask a different question: "How do I structure this loan to maximize my long-term advantage?" This book is designed to shift your mindset from approval-based thinking to strategy-based execution. It is not just about getting an SBA loan—it is about choosing the right SBA loan, structuring it correctly, and using it as a foundation for long-term financial growth.

At first glance, SBA mortgage loans may seem straightforward. You submit your financials, meet certain requirements, and receive financing based on your qualifications. However, beneath the surface lies a complex system of guidelines, risk assessments, interest rate calculations, and structural decisions that directly impact your monthly payments, cash flow, long-term equity, and overall profitability. Two borrowers with identical financial profiles can receive dramatically different outcomes based on how their loans are structured. One may struggle with high payments and limited flexibility, while the other may enjoy strong cash flow, tax advantages, and scalable growth opportunities. The difference lies in knowledge—and more importantly, in execution.

This book focuses on three core pillars: requirements, rates, and loan structures. Each of these elements plays a critical role in determining not only whether you qualify, but how favorable your loan terms will be. SBA loan requirements go far beyond basic credit scores and income verification. They include factors such as business experience, industry risk, property type, occupancy requirements, and the strength of your financial story. Understanding these requirements allows you to position yourself strategically before you ever submit an application. Instead of reacting to lender conditions, you will learn how to proactively build a borrower profile that attracts better terms and faster approvals.

Interest rates are often misunderstood, yet they are one of the most important components of any SBA mortgage loan. Many borrowers focus solely on the rate itself, without understanding how it is calculated or how it can change over time. SBA loans often use variable rate structures tied to benchmark indexes, combined with lender spreads that vary based on risk. This means that your rate is not just a number—it is a reflection of your risk profile, your deal structure, and your negotiation strategy. In this book, you will learn how rates are determined, how to evaluate different rate options, and how to choose between fixed and variable structures depending on your goals. More importantly, you will learn how to think beyond the rate and focus on total loan cost, payment stability, and long-term financial impact.

Loan structure is where strategy truly comes into play. This is where you decide how your loan will function over time. Will you prioritize lower monthly payments or faster equity buildup? Will you structure your loan to maximize cash flow or to minimize total interest paid? Will you choose longer amortization periods for flexibility, or shorter terms for aggressive payoff strategies? These decisions are not one-size-fits-all. They depend on your business model, your risk tolerance, your growth plans, and your exit strategy. A well-structured loan can provide the foundation for expansion, allowing you to reinvest cash flow into additional properties, new business opportunities, or operational improvements. A poorly structured loan, on the other hand, can limit your growth, create unnecessary financial pressure, and reduce your ability to adapt to changing market conditions.

One of the most powerful concepts you will learn in this book is how to compare SBA loan options effectively. Many borrowers assume that all SBA loans are similar, but this is far from the truth. SBA 7(a) loans and SBA 504 loans, for example, have fundamentally different structures, rate mechanisms, and use cases. Even within the same program, different lenders may offer different terms based on their risk appetite, internal guidelines, and market positioning. Learning how to analyze and compare these options allows you to choose the loan that aligns best with your objectives, rather than simply accepting the first approval you receive. This level of understanding gives you leverage—not just in choosing a loan, but in negotiating better terms.

Another key theme of this book is control. When you understand requirements, rates, and structures, you gain control over the lending process. You are no longer dependent on lenders to explain your options—you can evaluate them yourself. You can identify when a loan is structured in your favor and when it is not. You can ask better questions, negotiate more effectively, and make decisions with confidence. This level of control is what separates average borrowers from high-level operators. It allows you to move faster, reduce risk, and capitalize on opportunities that others may miss.

Throughout this book, we will also explore the relationship between financing and business strategy. Your loan is not just a financial obligation—it is a strategic tool that should align with your overall business plan. If your goal is to scale aggressively, your loan structure should support growth by preserving cash flow and maintaining flexibility. If your goal is stability and long-term ownership, your structure may prioritize fixed rates and predictable payments. If your goal is to acquire multiple properties, your financing strategy must consider how each loan impacts your ability to qualify for the next one. These are the types of strategic decisions that will define your success, and they all begin with a deep understanding of how SBA mortgage loans work.

This book is designed to be both practical and strategic. You will not only learn the technical aspects of SBA loan requirements, rate calculations, and structural options, but also how to apply this knowledge in real-world scenarios. You will see how different choices affect outcomes, how to avoid common mistakes, and how to position yourself for the best possible results. Whether you are purchasing your first commercial property, refinancing an existing loan, or planning a multi-property expansion, the principles in this book will help you make smarter, more informed decisions.

As you move through this book, you will begin to see SBA mortgage financing in a new light. Instead of viewing it as a complex and sometimes overwhelming process, you will start to recognize it as a powerful system that can be understood, optimized, and leveraged. You will develop the ability to break down loan offers, identify strengths and weaknesses, and choose the path that aligns with your long-term vision. This is the level of understanding that transforms financing from a necessity into a competitive advantage.

Ultimately, the goal of this book is to give you clarity. Clarity about what lenders are looking for, clarity about how rates are determined, and clarity about how to structure your loan for maximum benefit. With that clarity comes confidence—and with confidence comes the ability to act decisively. In the world of commercial real estate and business ownership, opportunities often move quickly. Those who are prepared, informed, and strategic are the ones who succeed.

By the end of this book, you will not only understand SBA mortgage loan requirements, rates, and structures—you will know how to use them. You will be equipped to compare options, make strategic decisions, and structure your financing in a way that supports your goals. Whether your objective is to build wealth, scale your business, or create long-term financial stability, the knowledge you gain here will serve as a foundation for everything that follows.

Chapter 1

Understanding SBA Mortgage Loan Requirements — Building a Strong Borrower Profile for Approval and Better Terms

When it comes to SBA mortgage financing, most borrowers focus on a single outcome: getting approved. However, approval is only the beginning. The real advantage lies in understanding the full scope of SBA loan requirements and using that knowledge to position yourself as a strong, low-risk borrower who qualifies not just for funding, but for the best possible terms. This chapter is designed to break down the key requirements that lenders evaluate and to help you understand how each component contributes to your overall borrower profile. By mastering these elements, you will shift from a reactive applicant to a strategic borrower who can influence outcomes before the application is even submitted.

At the core of SBA mortgage lending is risk assessment. Every lender is evaluating the likelihood that you will repay the loan as agreed, and this evaluation goes far beyond your credit score. While credit is important, it is only one piece of a much larger puzzle. Lenders analyze your personal financial strength, business performance, industry stability, management experience, and the quality of the real estate being financed. Each of these factors contributes to a comprehensive risk profile that ultimately determines your approval, interest rate, loan structure, and conditions. Understanding how these elements work together allows you to identify strengths, address weaknesses, and present a complete and compelling financial story.

One of the most important requirements in SBA mortgage lending is the concept of repayment ability. Lenders want to see clear, consistent cash flow that supports the loan payment with a comfortable margin. This is often measured using a debt service coverage ratio, or DSCR, which compares your available income to your total debt obligations. While the exact requirements may vary depending on the lender and the program, a DSCR above 1.25 is generally considered strong. This means that your income exceeds your debt obligations by at least 25 percent, providing a buffer that reduces the lender's risk. However, DSCR is not just about numbers—it is about how those numbers are presented. Clean, well-documented financials with clear explanations carry significantly more weight than disorganized or inconsistent records.

In addition to cash flow, lenders place significant emphasis on liquidity and reserves. SBA mortgage loans are long-term commitments, and lenders want to ensure that you have the financial capacity to handle unexpected challenges. This includes having sufficient cash reserves after closing to cover several months of loan payments, operating expenses, and potential vacancies or business fluctuations. Liquidity demonstrates financial discipline and provides reassurance that you can weather short-term disruptions without defaulting on the loan. Borrowers who maintain strong reserve positions are often viewed as lower risk, which can lead to more favorable terms and smoother approvals.

Another critical component of SBA loan requirements is borrower experience. Lenders want to see that you have the knowledge and ability to operate the business or manage the property being financed. This does not necessarily mean that you need decades of experience, but it does mean that your background should align with the proposed use of funds. For example, if you are purchasing an owner-occupied commercial property for your business, your experience in that industry becomes a key factor in the approval process. If you are acquiring a business along with real estate, lenders will evaluate your management capabilities and your ability to maintain or improve the performance of that business. Experience reduces uncertainty, and in lending, reduced uncertainty translates to reduced risk. Creditworthiness remains an essential requirement, but it should be viewed in context. A strong credit profile demonstrates a history of responsible financial behavior, but it is not the sole determinant of approval. SBA lenders often take a more holistic approach, considering compensating factors such as strong cash flow, significant liquidity, or extensive experience. This means that even borrowers with less-than-perfect credit may still qualify if they can demonstrate strength in other areas. However, improving your credit profile before applying can significantly enhance your positioning and open the door to better rates and terms.

The property itself also plays a crucial role in SBA mortgage loan requirements. Lenders evaluate the type, condition, location, and marketability of the property being financed. For owner-occupied properties, there are specific occupancy requirements that must be met, typically requiring that a significant portion of the property be used for the borrower's business operations. The property must also support the loan amount through its appraised value, ensuring that the lender has sufficient collateral. A well-located, well-maintained property in a stable market reduces risk and strengthens the overall loan profile.

Business financials are another key area of focus. Lenders review historical performance, including revenue, expenses, profitability, and trends over time. They are looking for consistency, growth potential, and the ability to sustain operations while servicing debt. If the business is newly established or undergoing changes, projections may be required to demonstrate future performance. These projections must be realistic, well-supported, and aligned with market conditions. Overly optimistic projections without supporting evidence can raise concerns, while conservative, well-documented projections can enhance credibility.

Personal financial strength is equally important. SBA loans often require personal guarantees, meaning that your personal financial position is directly tied to the loan. Lenders will review your personal income, assets, liabilities, and overall net worth. A strong personal financial profile provides additional assurance that you have the capacity to support the loan if needed. It also demonstrates commitment and alignment of interests, which are important factors in the lending decision.

Another often overlooked requirement is the quality of documentation. The way your financial information is presented can significantly impact the lender's perception of your application. Organized, accurate, and complete documentation reflects professionalism and attention to detail. It makes the underwriting process smoother and faster, reducing the likelihood of delays or additional conditions. On the other hand, incomplete or inconsistent documentation can create uncertainty, leading to more scrutiny and potentially less favorable terms.

As you begin to understand these requirements, it becomes clear that SBA mortgage lending is not just about meeting minimum standards—it is about building a strong, well-rounded borrower profile. Each component of your profile contributes to the overall risk assessment, and small improvements in multiple areas can have a significant cumulative impact. By taking a proactive approach, you can position yourself to not only qualify for financing but to secure terms that support your long-term goals.

Ultimately, mastering SBA loan requirements is about preparation and strategy. It is about understanding what lenders are looking for and aligning your financial profile accordingly. It is about anticipating questions, addressing potential concerns, and presenting a clear, compelling case for approval. When you approach the process with this level of understanding, you move from uncertainty to control. You become an informed borrower who can navigate the lending process with confidence and purpose.

As we move forward in this book, you will build on this foundation by exploring how interest rates are determined and how loan structures can be optimized. Together, these elements will give you the tools to not only secure SBA mortgage financing but to use it as a powerful driver of business growth and financial success.

Real-Life Math Example: Calculating Qualification, DSCR, and Loan Feasibility for an SBA Mortgage Loan

To fully understand how SBA mortgage loan requirements translate into real-world decisions, let's walk through a detailed example of a borrower evaluating a potential SBA-financed property purchase. Imagine a business owner named Michael who is purchasing a small commercial property for his operating business. The purchase price of the property is $1,200,000, and he plans to use an SBA loan with a 10 percent down payment. This means he will invest $120,000 of his own capital, and the loan amount will be $1,080,000.

The lender is offering a variable interest rate of 8.5 percent with a 25-year amortization. Based on these terms, Michael's estimated monthly loan payment is approximately $8,600. On an annual basis, this results in a total debt service of about $103,200. This number becomes critical because it will be used to evaluate whether the property and the business generate enough income to support the loan.

Michael's business currently generates a net operating income of $180,000 per year. To determine whether he meets the lender's DSCR requirement, we divide the net operating income by the annual debt service. In this case, $180,000 divided by $103,200 results in a DSCR of approximately 1.74. This is well above the typical minimum requirement of 1.25, indicating strong repayment ability. From a lender's perspective, this is a positive signal that the loan is likely to perform well.

However, the analysis does not stop there. The lender will also consider additional expenses associated with the property, such as property taxes, insurance, maintenance, and potential vacancies. Let's assume these additional expenses total $30,000 per year. When we subtract these expenses from the net operating income, Michael's adjusted income becomes $150,000. Now, when we calculate the DSCR using this adjusted figure, we divide $150,000 by $103,200, resulting in a DSCR of approximately 1.45. While still above the minimum requirement, this lower ratio provides a more realistic view of the loan's sustainability.

Next, we evaluate Michael's liquidity and reserves. After making the $120,000 down payment, he will have $200,000 remaining in liquid assets. The lender requires at least six months of reserves, which would be approximately $51,600 based on the monthly payment of $8,600. Since Michael has significantly more than this amount, he meets the reserve requirement comfortably. This strengthens his application and reduces perceived risk. We also examine Michael's personal debt obligations. He has a personal mortgage with a monthly payment of $2,000 and other debts totaling $1,000 per month. This adds $36,000 per year in personal debt obligations. While these do not directly impact the DSCR calculation for the business loan, they are considered in the overall risk assessment. Michael's strong income and liquidity help offset these obligations, maintaining a favorable profile.

Now let's explore how changes in interest rates could impact the deal. If the interest rate were to increase from 8.5 percent to 9.5 percent, the monthly payment would rise to approximately $9,400, increasing the annual debt service to $112,800. Using the adjusted income of $150,000, the new DSCR would be approximately 1.33. While still acceptable, the margin of safety has decreased. This highlights the importance of understanding rate sensitivity and choosing a structure that aligns with your risk tolerance.

Finally, we consider the long-term implications of the loan structure. With a 25-year amortization, Michael benefits from lower monthly payments, which supports cash flow. However, this also means that he will pay more interest over time compared to a shorter amortization period. If his goal is to maximize cash flow and reinvest in his business, this structure makes sense. If his goal were to minimize total interest and pay off the loan quickly, a shorter term might be more appropriate, even with higher monthly payments.

This example illustrates how multiple factors—income, expenses, reserves, interest rates, and loan structure—interact to determine whether a deal works. It also demonstrates the importance of analyzing not just whether you qualify, but how strong your position is and how sensitive your deal is to changes. By understanding these calculations and their implications, you can make more informed decisions, negotiate better terms, and structure your SBA mortgage loan in a way that supports your long-term success.

Chapter 2

Understanding SBA Mortgage Loan Interest Rates — How Rates Are Determined and How to Choose the Right Structure

Interest rates are one of the most critical components of any SBA mortgage loan, yet they are often misunderstood or oversimplified by borrowers. Many individuals focus only on the percentage itself, assuming that a lower rate automatically means a better deal. While rate is important, it is only one part of a much larger equation that includes loan structure, amortization, payment stability, and long-term cost. In SBA mortgage lending, interest rates are dynamic, influenced by multiple factors including market conditions, borrower risk, lender policies, and the specific SBA program being used. Understanding how these rates are built and how they behave over time is essential for making informed decisions that align with your financial goals.

At the foundation of most SBA mortgage loan rates is a benchmark index. For SBA 7(a) loans, this is commonly tied to the prime rate, which reflects the general cost of borrowing in the economy. The prime rate is influenced by broader economic factors, including monetary policy set by the Federal Reserve, inflation trends, and overall market conditions. On top of this base rate, lenders add a spread, which represents their margin and compensation for risk. This spread can vary depending on the strength of the borrower, the type of property, the loan amount, and the overall risk profile of the transaction. As a result, two borrowers applying for similar loans may receive different rates based on how lenders perceive their individual risk.

One of the most important distinctions in SBA mortgage loan rates is between variable and fixed rate structures. Variable rates adjust over time based on changes in the underlying index. For example, if your loan is tied to the prime rate and the prime rate increases, your interest rate—and therefore your monthly payment—will also increase. Variable rates often start lower than fixed rates, making them attractive for borrowers who prioritize lower initial payments. However, they also introduce uncertainty, as future rate movements can significantly impact affordability. Borrowers who choose variable rates must be prepared for potential fluctuations and should evaluate how changes in rates could affect their cash flow.

Fixed rates, on the other hand, provide stability and predictability. With a fixed rate structure, your interest rate remains constant for a specified period, or in some cases for the entire term of the loan. This allows you to plan with confidence, knowing that your monthly payment will not change due to interest rate movements. Fixed rates are commonly associated with SBA 504 loans, which are designed for long-term real estate financing with stable payments. While fixed rates may be slightly higher at the outset compared to variable rates, they offer protection against rising interest rates and can be particularly valuable in uncertain economic environments.

Another key concept in understanding SBA mortgage loan rates is rate caps and adjustments. Variable rate loans often include caps that limit how much the rate can increase over time or during a specific adjustment period. These caps provide a level of protection against extreme rate increases, but they do not eliminate the risk entirely. Borrowers must understand how frequently their rate can adjust, how much it can increase at each adjustment, and what the maximum rate could be over the life of the loan. This information is critical for evaluating worst-case scenarios and ensuring that the loan remains affordable even under less favorable conditions.

Beyond the rate itself, it is essential to consider the total cost of borrowing. This includes not only the interest paid over the life of the loan but also fees, closing costs, and prepayment penalties. SBA loans often include guaranty fees and other costs that can impact the overall expense of the loan. A slightly higher rate with lower fees may, in some cases, result in a lower total cost compared to a lower rate with higher upfront expenses. Evaluating the full financial picture allows you to make more informed comparisons and choose the option that provides the greatest long-term value.

Negotiation also plays a role in determining your interest rate. While SBA guidelines set maximum allowable spreads, lenders have flexibility within those limits. Borrowers with strong financial profiles, significant liquidity, and low-risk transactions may be able to negotiate more favorable terms. This is where preparation becomes critical. By presenting a well-organized, compelling application that highlights your strengths, you can position yourself as a desirable borrower and increase your leverage in rate discussions. Even small reductions in the interest rate can result in substantial savings over the life of the loan.

Timing is another factor that can influence your interest rate. Market conditions fluctuate, and interest rates can change based on economic trends, inflation expectations, and monetary policy decisions. While it is not always possible to predict these changes with certainty, being aware of the broader economic environment can help you make more strategic decisions about when to lock in a rate or move forward with a loan. In some cases, delaying a transaction in anticipation of lower rates may be beneficial, while in others, securing a rate early may protect you from future increases.

Loan term and amortization also interact with interest rates in important ways. A longer amortization period typically results in lower monthly payments but higher total interest paid over time. Conversely, a shorter amortization period increases monthly payments but reduces the total interest cost. The choice between these options depends on your financial objectives. If your priority is maximizing cash flow, a longer amortization with a manageable rate may be ideal. If your goal is to minimize long-term cost and build equity quickly, a shorter term may be more appropriate. Understanding how rate and term work together allows you to structure your loan in a way that supports your strategy.

It is also important to recognize that interest rates are a reflection of risk. Lenders price loans based on their assessment of how likely the borrower is to repay. Strong financials, consistent income, substantial reserves, and relevant experience all contribute to a lower perceived risk, which can lead to better rates. Conversely, higher risk profiles may result in higher rates to compensate the lender. This reinforces the importance of building a strong borrower profile, as discussed in the previous chapter. Your rate is not just determined by the market—it is influenced by how you present yourself as a borrower.

As you develop a deeper understanding of SBA mortgage loan interest rates, you begin to see that the rate itself is only one part of a broader strategy. The goal is not simply to obtain the lowest possible rate, but to choose a rate structure that aligns with your financial objectives, risk tolerance, and long-term plans. This may involve balancing lower initial payments with potential future increases, or accepting a slightly higher fixed rate in exchange for stability and predictability. Each decision should be made within the context of your overall strategy, ensuring that your financing supports your goals rather than limiting them.

Ultimately, mastering interest rates is about clarity and control. It is about understanding how rates are determined, how they behave over time, and how they interact with other elements of your loan. With this knowledge, you can evaluate options more effectively, negotiate with confidence, and make decisions that position you for long-term success. As we continue through this book, you will build on this foundation by exploring how loan structures can be optimized to further enhance your financial outcomes.

Real-Life Math Example: Comparing Variable vs Fixed Rates and Long-Term Loan Costs in an SBA Mortgage Loan

Let's walk through a detailed real-world scenario to understand how interest rates impact loan performance over time. Imagine a borrower named Sarah who is purchasing a commercial property for $2,000,000 using an SBA loan. She plans to put 10 percent down, which equals $200,000, resulting in a loan amount of $1,800,000. She is evaluating two options: a variable rate SBA 7(a) loan at 8.25 percent and a fixed rate SBA 504 loan at 8.75 percent.

For the variable rate option, Sarah receives a 25-year amortization. At an 8.25 percent interest rate, her monthly payment is approximately $14,400. This results in an annual debt service of about $172,800. Initially, this option appears attractive because of the lower rate and lower monthly payment. However, the rate is tied to the prime rate, which means it can change over time.

For the fixed rate option, the loan is structured with a blended SBA 504 structure, resulting in a fixed rate of 8.75 percent over 25 years. The monthly payment in this case is approximately $15,100, leading to an annual debt service of about $181,200. While the payment is higher, it remains stable for the life of the loan, providing predictability. Now let's analyze the long-term cost. Over 25 years, the total payments on the variable rate loan—assuming the rate never changes—would be approximately $4,320,000. Subtracting the original loan amount of $1,800,000, the total interest paid would be about $2,520,000. For the fixed rate loan, total payments would be approximately $4,530,000, resulting in total interest of about $2,730,000. At first glance, the variable rate loan appears to save Sarah $210,000 in interest.

However, this analysis assumes that the variable rate remains constant, which is unlikely. Let's consider a scenario where the rate increases by 1 percent after three years, rising from 8.25 percent to 9.25 percent. At this new rate, Sarah's monthly payment increases to approximately $15,800, raising her annual debt service to $189,600. Over time, this increase significantly impacts the total cost of the loan. If the rate continues to rise or remains elevated, the total interest paid could exceed that of the fixed rate option.

Next, we evaluate cash flow impact. Suppose Sarah's property generates a net operating income of $250,000 per year. With the variable rate loan at the initial rate, her DSCR is approximately 1.45 ($250,000 divided by $172,800). With the fixed rate loan, her DSCR is approximately 1.38 ($250,000 divided by $181,200). Both are acceptable, but the variable rate provides slightly more cash flow in the early years. Now consider the rate increase scenario. With the higher payment of $189,600, Sarah's DSCR drops to approximately 1.32. While still above minimum requirements, the margin has decreased, and her cash flow is tighter. This demonstrates how rate changes can affect not only total cost but also ongoing financial stability.

Finally, we examine strategic considerations. If Sarah plans to hold the property long-term and values stability, the fixed rate loan may be the better choice despite the higher initial cost. It protects her from rising rates and ensures predictable payments. If she plans to sell or refinance within a few years, the variable rate loan may offer short-term savings that align with her strategy.

This example highlights the importance of looking beyond the initial rate. By analyzing payment differences, total interest, rate sensitivity, and cash flow impact, Sarah can make a more informed decision that aligns with her goals. Understanding these dynamics allows borrowers to choose not just the cheapest option, but the smartest one for their specific situation.

Chapter 3

SBA Mortgage Loan Structures — How to Design the Right Loan for Cash Flow, Growth, and Long-Term Wealth

When most borrowers think about SBA mortgage loans, they tend to focus on approval and interest rates. However, one of the most powerful—and often overlooked—elements of SBA financing is loan structure. The way your loan is structured determines how your payments behave, how your cash flow performs, how quickly you build equity, and ultimately how much wealth you create over time. Two borrowers with identical loan amounts and interest rates can experience completely different financial outcomes based solely on how their loans are structured. This chapter is designed to help you understand how SBA mortgage loan structures work and how to design a structure that aligns with your business goals, investment strategy, and long-term vision.

At its core, loan structure refers to the combination of key components that define how your loan operates. These components include amortization period, loan term, payment type, rate structure, and any special features such as interest-only periods or balloon payments. Each of these elements affects your monthly payment, total interest cost, and financial flexibility. Understanding how these components interact allows you to move beyond generic loan options and create a customized financing strategy that supports your objectives.

One of the most important structural elements is amortization. Amortization determines how your loan balance is paid down over time. In SBA mortgage loans, amortization periods are typically long, often extending up to 25 years for real estate. A longer amortization results in lower monthly payments because the principal is spread out over a longer period. This improves cash flow, making it easier to manage operating expenses, reinvest in your business, or acquire additional assets. However, longer amortization also means that you pay more interest over time, as the loan balance declines more slowly. This trade-off between cash flow and total cost is one of the key decisions you must make when structuring your loan.

The loan term is another critical factor. While amortization determines how payments are calculated, the loan term defines how long the loan actually lasts before it must be paid off or refinanced. Some SBA loans, particularly SBA 7(a) loans, may have terms that align with the amortization period, while others may include shorter terms with longer amortization schedules, resulting in balloon payments. Understanding the difference between term and amortization is essential, as it affects your refinancing strategy, exit planning, and long-term financial obligations.

Payment structure is where flexibility and strategy come into play. Most SBA mortgage loans use fully amortizing payments, meaning each payment includes both principal and interest, gradually reducing the loan balance over time. However, some loans may offer interest-only periods, particularly in the early stages. During an interest-only period, your payments are lower because you are not paying down the principal. This can significantly improve cash flow in the short term, allowing you to stabilize a business, complete renovations, or invest in growth. However, once the interest-only period ends, payments increase as principal repayment begins. Borrowers must be prepared for this transition and ensure that their financial position can support the higher payments.

Another important structural decision involves how you balance cash flow versus equity growth. If your primary goal is to maximize monthly cash flow, you may choose a longer amortization period, potentially combined with an interest-only phase. This approach minimizes your monthly payment, freeing up capital for other uses. On the other hand, if your goal is to build equity quickly and reduce long-term interest costs, you may opt for a shorter amortization or make additional principal payments. This increases your monthly obligation but accelerates loan payoff and reduces total interest. Neither approach is inherently better—the right choice depends on your strategy and priorities.

SBA 7(a) and SBA 504 loans offer different structural advantages, and understanding these differences is key to making the right decision. SBA 7(a) loans are highly flexible, allowing for a wide range of uses, including real estate, business acquisition, and working capital. They typically feature variable rates and can include customized structures based on the borrower's needs. SBA 504 loans, on the other hand, are designed specifically for real estate and large equipment purchases. They offer long-term, fixed-rate financing through a unique structure that combines a bank loan with a government-backed debenture. This results in stable payments and predictable costs, making them ideal for borrowers who prioritize long-term stability.

Loan structure also plays a significant role in risk management. A well-structured loan can provide a buffer against economic uncertainty, allowing you to maintain financial stability even during challenging periods. For example, lower payments achieved through longer amortization can help you navigate temporary declines in revenue. Fixed-rate structures can protect you from rising

interest rates, ensuring that your payments remain manageable. By contrast, a poorly structured loan can expose you to unnecessary risk, such as payment shocks, refinancing pressure, or cash flow constraints.

Another key consideration is how your loan structure aligns with your exit strategy. Are you planning to hold the property long-term, sell it after a few years, or refinance once the business grows? Your loan structure should support this plan. For instance, if you intend to sell the property within five years, a loan with a longer amortization and lower payments may be advantageous, as it maximizes cash flow during the holding period. If you plan to hold the property indefinitely, a fixed-rate structure with predictable payments may be more appropriate. Aligning your loan structure with your exit strategy ensures that your financing supports your long-term goals rather than creating obstacles.

Prepayment considerations are another important aspect of loan structure. Some SBA loans include prepayment penalties, particularly in the early years. These penalties are designed to protect lenders from losing interest income if the loan is paid off early. Understanding these terms is essential, especially if you anticipate refinancing or selling the property. A loan with a lower rate but strict prepayment penalties may be less flexible than a slightly higher rate loan with more lenient terms. Evaluating these trade-offs allows you to choose a structure that provides both cost efficiency and flexibility.

As you begin to understand the nuances of SBA mortgage loan structures, it becomes clear that this is where strategic advantage is created. Structure is not just about how the loan is set up—it is about how the loan works for you over time. It is about designing a financial tool that supports your business, enhances your cash flow, and aligns with your long-term vision. By taking a thoughtful and informed approach, you can transform your loan from a simple financing arrangement into a powerful driver of growth and wealth creation.

Ultimately, mastering loan structure is about intentionality. It is about making deliberate choices based on your goals, rather than accepting default options. It is about understanding the trade-offs between cash flow and cost, flexibility and stability, short-term benefit and long-term impact. With this knowledge, you gain the ability to design a loan that works for you—not just today, but for years to come. As you continue through this book, you will build on this foundation, learning how to combine requirements, rates, and structures into a cohesive strategy that maximizes your success.

Real-Life Math Example: Structuring an SBA Mortgage Loan for Cash Flow vs Equity Growth

Let's walk through a detailed real-world scenario to understand how loan structure impacts financial outcomes. Imagine a borrower named David who is purchasing a commercial property for $1,500,000. He puts down 10 percent, or $150,000, resulting in a loan amount of $1,350,000. He is evaluating two different loan structures with the same interest rate of 8.5 percent but different amortization strategies.

Option one is a 25-year amortization with fully amortizing payments. Under this structure, David's monthly payment is approximately $10,400, resulting in an annual debt service of about $124,800. This lower payment provides strong cash flow, allowing David to reinvest in his business or maintain higher reserves.

Option two is a more aggressive structure with a 20-year amortization. In this case, the monthly payment increases to approximately $11,700, with an annual debt service of about $140,400. While this higher payment reduces cash flow, it accelerates principal repayment and reduces total interest over time.

Now let's compare the long-term impact. Over 25 years, the total payments for option one would be approximately $3,120,000, meaning David pays about $1,770,000 in interest. For option two, over 20 years, total payments would be approximately $2,808,000, resulting in about $1,458,000 in interest. This means that by choosing the shorter amortization, David saves approximately $312,000 in interest. However, this savings comes at the cost of reduced cash flow. The difference in monthly payments between the two options is $1,300. Over a year, this amounts to $15,600. If David could reinvest this $15,600 annually into his business at a return of 10 percent, the opportunity cost of choosing the higher payment structure could be significant over time.

Next, let's introduce a third option: a 25-year amortization with a 3-year interest-only period. During the interest-only phase, David's monthly payment drops to approximately $9,560, resulting in annual payments of about $114,720. This provides even greater cash flow in the early years, which could be used to stabilize operations or fund growth initiatives. However, once the interest-only period ends, the payment increases to the fully amortizing level of $10,400.

Now let's evaluate cash flow using a net operating income of $180,000 per year. Under option one, the DSCR is approximately 1.44 ($180,000 divided by $124,800). Under option two, the DSCR drops to approximately 1.28 ($180,000 divided by $140,400). Under the interest-only structure, the DSCR during the initial period is approximately 1.57 ($180,000 divided by $114,720), providing the strongest short-term cash flow. This example highlights the trade-offs between different structures. The longer amortization and interest-only options provide better cash flow, which can support growth and flexibility. The shorter amortization reduces total interest and builds equity faster but requires higher payments. The right choice depends on David's strategy. If he plans to expand his business and needs cash flow, the longer amortization or interest-only option may be more beneficial. If his goal is to minimize interest and build equity quickly, the shorter amortization may be the better choice.

Finally, consider the impact of early payoff. If David chooses option one but makes additional principal payments of $500 per month, he can significantly reduce the loan term and interest cost without committing to a higher required payment. This hybrid approach combines flexibility with efficiency, allowing him to adjust his strategy based on performance.

This real-life example demonstrates how loan structure directly influences financial outcomes. By analyzing payments, interest, cash flow, and flexibility, David can choose the structure that best aligns with his goals. Understanding these dynamics empowers borrowers to make strategic decisions that go beyond basic approval, turning financing into a powerful tool for long-term success.

Chapter 4

Comparing SBA Mortgage Loan Options – Choosing the Right Loan for Your Strategy

Choosing between SBA mortgage loan options is one of the most important decisions a borrower will make, yet it is often approached with limited understanding or rushed judgment. Many borrowers assume that once they are approved, the process is complete and the best path forward is simply to move ahead with the loan offered. However, experienced borrowers understand that approval is only the beginning. The real advantage lies in comparing options strategically and selecting the loan that aligns with long-term goals, cash flow needs, and growth plans. This chapter is designed to help you develop a framework for comparing SBA mortgage loan options so you can make decisions that maximize both short-term performance and long-term financial success.

At the center of SBA mortgage financing are two primary programs: SBA 7(a) and SBA 504. While both are backed by the Small Business Administration and designed to support business growth, they are fundamentally different in structure, flexibility, and use case. The SBA 7(a) loan is known for its versatility. It can be used for real estate, business acquisition, refinancing, working capital, and more. It typically features a single loan with a variable interest rate and flexible terms. This makes it an excellent option for borrowers who need adaptability and a broader range of financing uses.

In contrast, the SBA 504 loan is specifically designed for fixed assets such as commercial real estate and large equipment. It uses a dual-loan structure, combining a bank loan (typically 50 percent of the project) with a government-backed debenture (typically 40 percent), while the borrower contributes around 10 percent. One of the biggest advantages of the SBA 504 program is its fixed-rate component, which provides long-term stability and predictable payments. This makes it particularly attractive for borrowers who prioritize certainty and want to lock in financing over an extended period.

When comparing these options, the first step is to clearly define your objective. Are you purchasing owner-occupied real estate? Acquiring a business? Refinancing existing debt? Expanding operations? Each of these scenarios may favor a different loan type. For example, if you are buying a business that includes real estate and need working capital as part of the transaction, an SBA 7(a) loan may be more suitable due to its flexibility. If your primary goal is to purchase or refinance commercial real estate with stable, long-term payments, an

SBA 504 loan may offer significant advantages.

Another key factor in comparison is interest rate structure. SBA 7(a) loans typically use variable rates tied to an index such as the prime rate, while SBA 504 loans offer fixed rates on the debenture portion. This difference has a major impact on payment stability and long-term cost. Variable rates may start lower, providing immediate savings, but they introduce uncertainty as rates can increase over time. Fixed rates may be slightly higher initially but offer protection against future rate increases. Understanding your risk tolerance and financial capacity is essential when evaluating these options.

Loan structure also plays a critical role in comparison. SBA 7(a) loans are generally simpler, with a single lender and a single payment. SBA 504 loans involve two lenders and two payments, which can add complexity but also provide structural benefits. The blended rate of an SBA 504 loan can be competitive, and the fixed-rate portion provides stability. Additionally, the longer amortization periods available in both programs can significantly impact monthly payments and cash flow.

Cash flow is often one of the most important considerations for borrowers. Lower monthly payments provide greater flexibility, allowing you to reinvest in your business, manage unexpected expenses, or pursue additional opportunities. When comparing loan options, it is important to look beyond the rate and evaluate the actual monthly payment and how it fits within your overall financial picture. A loan with a slightly higher rate but a longer amortization may result in a lower payment and better cash flow, which could be more beneficial in the long run.

Another important aspect of comparison is total loan cost. This includes not only interest but also fees, closing costs, and any additional expenses associated with the loan. SBA loans often include guaranty fees, which vary based on the loan amount and structure. These costs can impact the overall economics of the deal and should be factored into your analysis. Comparing total cost rather than just interest rate provides a more accurate picture of which loan is truly more advantageous.

Flexibility is another critical factor. SBA 7(a) loans offer more flexibility in terms of use of funds, prepayment options, and structuring. SBA 504 loans, while more limited in use, provide stability and long-term predictability. If your strategy involves frequent refinancing, repositioning, or selling in the short term, flexibility may be more important. If your goal is long-term ownership and stable operations, predictability may be the priority.

Prepayment terms are also an important consideration. Some SBA loans include prepayment penalties, particularly in the early years. These penalties can impact your ability to refinance or sell the property without incurring additional costs. Understanding these terms is essential when comparing options, especially if you anticipate changes in your strategy over time.

Another often overlooked factor is lender experience and execution. Not all lenders approach SBA loans in the same way. Some lenders specialize in SBA 7(a) loans, while others focus on SBA 504 financing. The lender's experience, efficiency, and willingness to structure deals creatively can have a significant impact on your outcome. A slightly higher rate with a highly experienced lender who can close quickly and structure the deal effectively may be more valuable than a lower rate with a less experienced lender.

As you compare SBA mortgage loan options, it is important to take a holistic approach. This means evaluating not just individual components, but how they work together as part of a complete financing strategy. The goal is not simply to find the cheapest loan, but to find the loan that best supports your objectives. This may involve balancing competing priorities such as cost, flexibility, stability, and growth potential.

Ultimately, the ability to compare SBA loan options effectively is a powerful skill. It allows you to make informed decisions, negotiate better terms, and structure your financing in a way that aligns with your vision. Instead of being limited by the options presented to you, you become an active participant in the process, capable of shaping your own financial future.

As you continue through this book, you will build on this foundation, learning how to combine requirements, rates, and structures into a cohesive strategy. By mastering these elements, you will not only be able to secure SBA mortgage financing, but also use it as a strategic tool to achieve your goals.

Real-Life Math Example: Comparing SBA 7(a) vs SBA 504 Loan Options

Let's walk through a detailed example to understand how to compare SBA loan options in a real-world scenario. Imagine a borrower named Carlos who is purchasing a commercial property for $2,500,000. He is evaluating two options: an SBA 7(a) loan and an SBA 504 loan.

For the SBA 7(a) option, Carlos puts down 10 percent, or $250,000, resulting in a loan amount of $2,250,000. The interest rate is 8.25 percent with a 25-year amortization. His monthly payment is approximately $17,300, resulting in an annual debt service of about $207,600.

For the SBA 504 option, the structure is split into two loans. The bank finances 50 percent, or $1,250,000, at a variable rate of 7.75 percent. The SBA finances 40 percent, or $1,000,000, at a fixed rate of 8.75 percent. Carlos contributes the same $250,000 down payment. The combined monthly payment for both loans is approximately $16,900, resulting in an annual debt service of about $202,800.

At first glance, the SBA 504 option appears slightly more favorable in terms of monthly payment, saving Carlos about $400 per month. Over a year, this amounts to $4,800 in savings. Over 25 years, assuming rates remain constant, this difference becomes significant.

Now let's evaluate total cost. For the SBA 7(a) loan, total payments over 25 years are approximately $5,190,000, resulting in total interest of about $2,940,000. For the SBA 504 loan, total payments are approximately $5,070,000, resulting in total interest of about $2,820,000. This means the SBA 504 option saves Carlos approximately $120,000 in total interest.

Next, consider rate risk. The SBA 7(a) loan has a fully variable rate, meaning the payment could increase if rates rise. The

SBA 504 loan has a partially fixed rate, providing some protection against rate increases. If rates rise by 1 percent, Carlos's payment on the SBA 7(a) loan could increase to approximately $18,700 per month, significantly impacting cash flow. The SBA 504 loan would see a smaller increase due to its fixed component.

Now let's evaluate cash flow. Suppose the property generates a net operating income of $300,000 per year. For the SBA 7(a) loan, the DSCR is approximately 1.44 ($300,000 divided by $207,600). For the SBA 504 loan, the DSCR is approximately 1.48 ($300,000 divided by $202,800). Both are strong, but the SBA 504 loan provides slightly better coverage.

Finally, consider flexibility. The SBA 7(a) loan allows Carlos to include working capital and other expenses in the loan, while the SBA 504 loan is limited to fixed assets. If Carlos needs additional funds for business operations, the SBA 7(a) loan may be more suitable despite the higher cost.

This example demonstrates how multiple factors—payment, total cost, rate risk, cash flow, and flexibility—must be considered when comparing SBA loan options. By analyzing each of these elements, Carlos can make a decision that aligns with his goals, whether that is minimizing cost, maximizing stability, or maintaining flexibility.

Chapter 5

Optimizing SBA Mortgage Loan Terms — Negotiation Strategies, Cost Control, and Long-Term Financial Positioning

Once you understand SBA mortgage loan requirements, interest rates, and loan structures, the next level of mastery comes from optimization. This is where you move beyond simply accepting loan terms and begin actively shaping them to serve your financial strategy. Optimization is not about finding a perfect loan—because no such loan exists—but about improving each component of the loan to create the best possible outcome based on your goals. In this chapter, we will explore how to negotiate SBA mortgage loan terms, reduce total borrowing costs, and position yourself for long-term financial success.

Most borrowers underestimate how much control they have in the loan process. While SBA guidelines establish certain boundaries, lenders have flexibility within those limits. This flexibility applies to interest rate spreads, fee structures, amortization choices, and even certain conditions of the loan. Borrowers who understand this dynamic can use it to their advantage. The key is preparation. A well-prepared borrower with strong financials, clear documentation, and a compelling narrative is far more likely to receive favorable terms than one who approaches the process passively.

Negotiation begins with understanding what drives lender decisions. Lenders are primarily concerned with risk and return. If you can demonstrate that your loan represents low risk—through strong cash flow, high liquidity, relevant experience, and a solid property—you reduce the lender's need to price in additional risk. This can translate into lower interest rate spreads, reduced fees, and more flexible terms. On the other hand, higher perceived risk leads to tighter conditions and higher costs. This means that improving your borrower profile is one of the most effective negotiation strategies available.

One of the most impactful areas for negotiation is the interest rate spread. While the base rate may be tied to an index such as prime, the spread added by the lender can vary. Even a small reduction in the spread can result in significant savings over time. For example, reducing your rate by just 0.25 percent on a large loan can save tens or even hundreds of thousands of dollars over the life of the loan. This is why it is important to shop multiple lenders and create competitive pressure. When lenders know they are competing for your business, they are more likely to offer favorable terms. Fees are another area where optimization can have a meaningful impact. SBA loans often include guaranty fees, packaging fees, and closing costs. While some of these are fixed or regulated, others may be negotiable or subject to variation between lenders. Understanding which fees are mandatory and which are flexible allows you to focus your negotiation efforts effectively. In some cases, lenders may be willing to reduce or offset certain fees to win your business, especially if you are a strong borrower.

Amortization and loan term are also important levers in optimization. As discussed in previous chapters, longer amortization periods reduce monthly payments but increase total interest, while shorter periods do the opposite. The optimal choice depends on your strategy. However, you can often negotiate terms that provide flexibility, such as the ability to make additional principal payments without penalty. This allows you to benefit from lower required payments while still having the option to reduce your loan balance more quickly when cash flow allows.

Prepayment terms are another critical consideration. Many SBA loans include prepayment penalties, particularly in the early years. These penalties can limit your ability to refinance or sell the property without incurring additional costs. However, not all loans have the same prepayment structures.

Some may have declining penalties over time, while others may be more restrictive. Understanding these terms and negotiating for more favorable conditions can provide valuable flexibility, especially if your long-term plans include refinancing or selling.

Another powerful optimization strategy involves structuring your loan to align with your business cycle. For example, if your business is seasonal or expected to grow over time, you may benefit from a structure that provides lower payments in the early years. This could include an interest-only period or a longer amortization. As your income increases, you can then accelerate repayment. Aligning your loan structure with your cash flow patterns ensures that your financing supports your operations rather than creating unnecessary pressure.

Cash flow optimization is one of the most important goals in SBA mortgage financing. Strong cash flow provides flexibility, reduces stress, and creates opportunities for growth. When evaluating loan terms, it is important to consider how each component affects your monthly payment and overall financial position. A loan with slightly higher total cost but significantly better cash flow may be more advantageous if it allows you to invest in your business, acquire additional properties, or build reserves.

Another key aspect of optimization is understanding the trade-offs between short-term and long-term benefits. Lower payments today may result in higher total costs over time, while higher payments may reduce long-term expenses but limit your flexibility. The right balance depends on your goals. If you are focused on growth and expansion, prioritizing cash flow may be the best approach. If you are focused on stability and long-term wealth accumulation, minimizing interest and building equity may take precedence.

Refinancing strategy should also be considered during the initial loan structuring process. Many borrowers think of refinancing as a future decision, but it is important to plan for it from the beginning. This includes understanding prepayment terms, market conditions, and how your financial profile is likely to evolve over time. Structuring your loan in a way that allows for future refinancing can provide significant advantages, especially if interest rates decline or your business performance improves.

Lender selection is another critical component of optimization. Not all lenders approach SBA loans in the same way. Some are more conservative, while others are more flexible and creative. Some prioritize speed and efficiency, while others focus on relationship building. Choosing the right lender can have a significant impact on your experience and outcome. A lender who understands your goals and is willing to work with you can provide value beyond just the loan terms. As you begin to apply these optimization strategies, you will notice a shift in how you approach SBA mortgage financing. Instead of reacting to offers, you will start to shape them. Instead of focusing on individual components, you will evaluate the entire loan as a strategic tool. This shift in mindset is what separates average borrowers from high-level operators.

Ultimately, optimizing your SBA mortgage loan is about maximizing value. It is about reducing unnecessary costs, increasing flexibility, and aligning your financing with your long-term objectives. By taking a proactive and strategic approach, you can turn your loan into a powerful asset that supports your growth and enhances your financial position.

As you move forward, remember that every decision you make in the loan process has a compounding effect. Small improvements in rate, structure, or terms can lead to significant differences over time. By focusing on optimization, you ensure that your financing works for you—not against you—creating a foundation for long-term success.

Real-Life Math Example: Negotiating and Optimizing an SBA Mortgage Loan for Maximum Savings and Cash Flow

Let's walk through a detailed real-world example to see how optimization strategies can impact a borrower's financial outcome. Imagine a borrower named Elena who is purchasing a commercial property for $3,000,000. She plans to put down 10 percent, or $300,000, resulting in a loan amount of $2,700,000.

Elena receives an initial loan offer with an interest rate of 8.75 percent and a 25-year amortization. Her monthly payment is approximately $21,600, resulting in an annual debt service of about $259,200. Over 25 years, her total payments would be approximately $6,480,000, meaning she would pay about $3,780,000 in interest.

Before accepting the offer, Elena shops multiple lenders and negotiates a reduction in the interest rate to 8.5 percent. This small reduction lowers her monthly payment to approximately $20,800, saving her $800 per month. On an annual basis, this is a savings of $9,600. Over 25 years, this reduction results in total savings of approximately $240,000 in interest.

Next, Elena negotiates her fee structure. The original loan included $60,000 in total fees. By comparing lenders and leveraging her strong financial profile, she reduces these fees to $45,000, saving an additional $15,000 upfront.

Now let's explore amortization optimization. Elena considers switching to a 20-year amortization, which would increase her monthly payment to approximately $23,500 but reduce total interest to about $3,240,000. This would save her approximately $540,000 in interest compared to the original 25-year structure. However, the higher payment would reduce her cash flow.

Instead, Elena chooses a hybrid approach. She keeps the 25-year amortization for flexibility but commits to making an additional $1,000 per month in principal payments. This increases her effective monthly payment to $21,800 but allows her to pay off the loan in approximately 21 years instead of 25. As a result, she saves approximately $400,000 in interest while maintaining the option to reduce payments if needed.

Now let's evaluate cash flow. Suppose Elena's property generates a net operating income of $400,000 per year. With her optimized payment of $21,800 per month, her annual debt service is $261,600, resulting in a DSCR of approximately 1.53. This provides strong cash flow and a comfortable margin above lender requirements.

Finally, Elena negotiates prepayment terms, reducing the penalty period from five years to three years with a declining structure. This gives her the flexibility to refinance if rates drop or if her business performance improves.

This example demonstrates how multiple small optimizations—rate reduction, fee negotiation, amortization strategy, and prepayment flexibility—can combine to create significant financial benefits. Elena not only reduces her total borrowing cost by hundreds of thousands of dollars but also improves her cash flow and maintains flexibility.

By applying these strategies, borrowers can transform their SBA mortgage loans into highly efficient financial tools. Instead of accepting standard terms, they can actively shape their financing to align with their goals, maximize savings, and support long-term success.

Chapter 6

Managing Risk in SBA Mortgage Loans – Protecting Cash Flow, Stability, and Long-Term Success

As you progress in your understanding of SBA mortgage financing, one of the most critical concepts to master is risk management. While approval, rates, and loan structures determine how a deal looks on paper, risk management determines how that deal performs over time—especially during uncertainty. Many borrowers focus on getting the deal done, but experienced operators focus on ensuring the deal survives and thrives under different conditions. This chapter is designed to help you identify, measure, and manage the risks associated with SBA mortgage loans so you can protect your cash flow, maintain stability, and position yourself for long-term success.

Risk in SBA mortgage lending comes from multiple sources. The most obvious is financial risk—the possibility that your income may decline or your expenses may increase, making it more difficult to meet your loan obligations. However, there are also interest rate risks, operational risks, market risks, and structural risks embedded within the loan itself.

Understanding these risks is the first step toward managing them effectively. When you recognize where vulnerabilities exist, you can take proactive steps to reduce their impact.

One of the most important risk factors is cash flow variability. Your ability to service your loan depends on consistent income, but businesses and properties rarely perform in a perfectly stable manner. Revenues may fluctuate due to seasonality, economic conditions, competition, or operational challenges. At the same time, expenses may increase unexpectedly due to maintenance, labor costs, or external factors. This is why lenders require a buffer in the form of a strong debt service coverage ratio. However, as a borrower, you should aim for an even stronger margin than the minimum required. A DSCR of 1.25 may satisfy a lender, but a DSCR of 1.40 or higher provides a much greater cushion against unexpected changes.

Liquidity is another critical component of risk management. Cash reserves act as your safety net, allowing you to continue making payments even if your income temporarily declines. Without sufficient reserves, even a short-term disruption can create significant stress. A common guideline is to maintain at least six to twelve months of reserves, but the appropriate level depends on your risk tolerance and the nature of your business. Strong liquidity not only protects you during challenging periods but also provides flexibility to take advantage of opportunities.

Interest rate risk is particularly relevant for SBA 7(a) loans, which often use variable rate structures. As discussed in earlier chapters, variable rates can change over time, increasing your monthly payment. This creates uncertainty and can impact your cash flow if rates rise significantly. Managing this risk involves understanding how your rate is structured, evaluating potential rate scenarios, and ensuring that your financial position can support higher payments if necessary. In some cases, choosing a fixed-rate structure or refinancing into one may be a way to reduce this risk.

Operational risk is another important consideration. This refers to your ability to successfully manage the business or property associated with the loan. Even with strong financials, poor management decisions can lead to declining performance and increased risk. This is why lenders place such emphasis on borrower experience. As a borrower, you should continually evaluate your operations, identify areas for improvement, and ensure that your business is positioned for long-term success. Strong operations reduce risk and enhance your ability to meet your financial obligations.

Market risk is also a factor that cannot be ignored. Changes in the broader economy, industry trends, and local market conditions can all impact your business and property value. While you cannot control these factors, you can prepare for them. This includes choosing properties in stable or growing markets, diversifying your income sources, and avoiding over-leveraging. A conservative approach to leverage—meaning not borrowing to the absolute maximum—can provide additional protection against market fluctuations.

Loan structure itself can introduce risk if not designed carefully. For example, loans with interest-only periods may provide short-term relief but can lead to payment shocks when the amortization begins. Similarly, loans with balloon payments may require refinancing at a future date, exposing you to market conditions at that time. Understanding these structural elements and planning accordingly is essential for managing long-term risk.

Another key aspect of risk management is stress testing your loan. This involves evaluating how your loan performs under different scenarios. For example, what happens if your income decreases by 10 percent? What if your expenses increase by 15 percent? What if interest rates rise by 1 or 2 percent? By running these scenarios, you can identify potential weaknesses and take steps to address them before they become real problems. Stress testing transforms uncertainty into actionable insight. Insurance and contingency planning also play a role in managing risk. Adequate property insurance, business interruption coverage, and liability protection can help mitigate financial losses in the event of unforeseen events. Additionally, having a clear contingency plan—such as access to additional capital or alternative revenue streams—can provide a path forward during challenging times.

Another important concept is diversification. Relying on a single source of income or a single property can increase risk. By diversifying your investments, income streams, or business operations, you reduce your exposure to any one factor. This can enhance stability and improve your overall financial resilience.

As you manage risk, it is important to strike a balance between caution and opportunity. While minimizing risk is important, excessive caution can limit growth. The goal is not to eliminate risk entirely—because that is impossible—but to manage it intelligently. This means taking calculated risks that align with your goals while maintaining safeguards that protect your downside.

Ultimately, risk management is about control and preparedness. It is about understanding the variables that can impact your loan and taking proactive steps to address them. By doing so, you position yourself to navigate challenges with confidence and maintain stability even in uncertain conditions.

As you continue through this book, you will see how risk management integrates with all aspects of SBA mortgage financing. By combining strong requirements, optimized rates, strategic structures, and effective risk management, you create a comprehensive approach that supports both immediate success and long-term growth.

Real-Life Math Example: Stress Testing an SBA Mortgage Loan for Risk and Stability

Let's walk through a detailed real-world example to understand how risk management and stress testing work in practice. Imagine a borrower named Jason who has secured an SBA loan of $2,200,000 at an interest rate of 8.5 percent with a 25-year amortization. His monthly payment is approximately $17,000, resulting in an annual debt service of $204,000.

Jason's business generates a net operating income of $300,000 per year. This results in a DSCR of approximately 1.47 ($300,000 divided by $204,000), which is strong and provides a comfortable margin. However, Jason wants to understand how his loan would perform under different risk scenarios.

First, he evaluates a decline in income. If his income decreases by 15 percent, his new income would be $255,000. Dividing this by the annual debt service of $204,000 results in a DSCR of approximately 1.25. While still acceptable, the margin has significantly decreased, indicating that his loan is more sensitive to income fluctuations than it initially appeared.

Next, Jason evaluates an increase in expenses. If his expenses increase by $30,000 per year, his adjusted income becomes $270,000. This results in a DSCR of approximately 1.32. This scenario shows that rising costs can also impact his financial position, even if revenue remains stable.

Now, Jason considers interest rate risk. If his variable rate increases from 8.5 percent to 9.5 percent, his monthly payment would rise to approximately $18,800, increasing his annual debt service to $225,600. Using his original income of $300,000, his DSCR would drop to approximately 1.33. If this rate increase were combined with a 10 percent income decline, his DSCR would fall to approximately 1.20, which could create challenges in maintaining financial stability.

Jason also evaluates his liquidity. After closing, he has $250,000 in reserves. His monthly payment is $17,000, meaning he has approximately 14 months of reserves. This provides a strong safety net, allowing him to manage temporary disruptions without defaulting on the loan.

Finally, Jason considers a worst-case scenario where income declines by 20 percent and interest rates increase by 1 percent. In this case, his income would be $240,000, and his annual debt service would be $225,600. This results in a DSCR of approximately 1.06, which is very tight and indicates a high level of risk. However, his strong reserves provide a buffer, allowing him to continue making payments while addressing the underlying issues.

This example demonstrates how stress testing can reveal potential vulnerabilities and help borrowers prepare for different scenarios. By understanding how changes in income, expenses, and interest rates affect his loan, Jason can take proactive steps to strengthen his position. This might include increasing reserves, reducing expenses, or exploring fixed-rate options.

Through this process, Jason transforms uncertainty into insight, allowing him to manage risk effectively and maintain control over his financial future.

Chapter 7

Scaling with SBA Mortgage Loans — Using Financing to Build a Portfolio and Expand Your Business

Once you understand how SBA mortgage loans work—requirements, rates, structures, optimization, and risk management—the next level is using these loans as a strategic tool to scale. This is where financing transitions from a one-time transaction into a repeatable system for growth. Many borrowers use SBA loans to acquire a single property or business and stop there. However, sophisticated operators use SBA financing as a stepping stone to build portfolios, expand operations, and create long-term wealth. This chapter is focused on showing you how to think beyond one deal and begin designing a scalable strategy using SBA mortgage loans.

Scaling with SBA financing starts with a shift in mindset. Instead of asking, "Can I qualify for this loan?" you begin asking, "How does this loan position me for the next one?" Every decision you make—from how you structure your loan to how you manage cash flow—should be evaluated in terms of its impact on future opportunities. This means thinking strategically about debt, income, reserves, and how each deal affects your overall financial profile. The goal is to create a system where each successful deal strengthens your ability to execute the next one.

One of the most important concepts in scaling is preserving borrowing capacity. SBA loans often require personal guarantees and consider your global cash flow when evaluating new applications. This means that your existing loans can impact your ability to qualify for additional financing. To scale effectively, you must manage your debt in a way that maintains strong coverage ratios and demonstrates consistent performance. This includes avoiding over-leveraging, maintaining strong cash flow, and ensuring that each deal contributes positively to your overall financial position.

Cash flow is the engine of scaling. Strong, consistent cash flow not only supports your current obligations but also provides the capital needed for future investments. When structuring your SBA mortgage loans, prioritizing cash flow can create a foundation for growth. This may involve choosing longer amortization periods, negotiating favorable rates, or structuring payments in a way that aligns with your business cycle. The more cash flow you generate, the more flexibility you have to reinvest, build reserves, and pursue additional opportunities. Another key factor in scaling is equity growth. As you pay down your loan and as your property or business increases in value, you build equity. This equity can be leveraged in the future through refinancing or additional financing. Understanding how to balance cash flow and equity growth is essential. While aggressive principal repayment builds equity faster, it may reduce cash flow that could otherwise be used for expansion. Conversely, maximizing cash flow may slow equity growth but provide the resources needed to scale more quickly. The right balance depends on your strategy and timeline.

Refinancing plays a critical role in scaling. As your business grows and your financial profile improves, you may have opportunities to refinance your SBA loan into more favorable terms. This could include lower interest rates, longer amortization periods, or even transitioning into conventional financing. Refinancing can reduce your monthly payments, improve cash flow, and free up capital for additional investments. Planning for refinancing from the beginning allows you to structure your initial loan in a way that supports future transitions.

Portfolio strategy is another essential component of scaling. Instead of viewing each property or business as an isolated investment, you should think in terms of a portfolio. This means considering how each asset contributes to your overall financial picture. Diversification can reduce risk and enhance stability, while strategic alignment can create synergies between assets. For example, owning multiple properties in complementary markets or operating businesses that support each other can strengthen your overall position.

Timing is also critical in scaling. Moving too quickly can lead to over-leverage and increased risk, while moving too slowly can result in missed opportunities. The key is to find a pace that allows you to grow sustainably while maintaining financial stability. This often involves reinvesting profits, building reserves, and carefully evaluating each new opportunity. By maintaining discipline and focusing on long-term goals, you can create a steady and sustainable growth trajectory.

Another important consideration is operational scalability. As you acquire more properties or expand your business, your operational complexity increases. This requires systems, processes, and potentially additional personnel to manage effectively. Ensuring that your operations can scale alongside your financing is essential for maintaining performance and minimizing risk. Strong operations support strong financial performance, which in turn supports continued access to financing.

Relationships also play a significant role in scaling. Building strong relationships with lenders, brokers, and financial professionals can provide access to better opportunities and more favorable terms. Lenders who understand your track record and trust your ability to perform are more likely to support your growth. Maintaining transparency, delivering consistent results, and communicating effectively can strengthen these relationships and enhance your ability to scale.

As you begin to scale, it is important to maintain a long-term perspective. Short-term gains should not come at the expense of long-term stability. This means avoiding excessive risk, maintaining adequate reserves, and ensuring that each decision aligns with your overall strategy. Scaling is not just about acquiring more assets—it is about building a sustainable system that generates consistent income and long-term wealth.

Another powerful concept in scaling is compounding. As your portfolio grows, the benefits of each additional asset begin to compound. Cash flow from multiple properties can be reinvested to acquire new assets, creating a cycle of growth. Over time, this compounding effect can lead to significant wealth creation. However, this only works if each deal is structured and managed effectively.

Ultimately, scaling with SBA mortgage loans is about leveraging financing as a tool for growth. It is about using each loan to build momentum, strengthen your financial position, and create opportunities for the future. By approaching each deal strategically and maintaining a focus on long-term goals, you can transform SBA financing into a powerful engine for expansion.

As you move forward, remember that scaling is a process. It requires patience, discipline, and continuous learning. By applying the principles in this chapter, you can build a foundation for sustainable growth and position yourself for long-term success.

Real-Life Math Example: Scaling from One SBA Loan to a Portfolio of Properties

Let's walk through a detailed example to understand how scaling works in practice. Imagine a borrower named Daniel who starts with a single SBA-financed property. He purchases a property for $1,800,000 with a 10 percent down payment of $180,000, resulting in a loan amount of $1,620,000. The interest rate is 8.5 percent with a 25-year amortization, leading to a monthly payment of approximately $12,500, or $150,000 annually.

Daniel's property generates a net operating income of

$240,000 per year. This results in a DSCR of 1.60 ($240,000 divided by $150,000), which is strong. After expenses and loan payments, Daniel has approximately $90,000 in annual cash flow.

Instead of spending this cash flow, Daniel reinvests it. After two years, he has accumulated $180,000 in additional capital. Combined with his initial reserves and some appreciation in property value, he is able to pursue a second property.

For the second property, Daniel purchases another building for $2,000,000 with a 10 percent down payment of $200,000. The loan amount is $1,800,000 at an interest rate of 8.75 percent, resulting in a monthly payment of approximately $14,200, or $170,400 annually. This property generates a net operating income of $280,000, resulting in a DSCR of approximately 1.64.

Now Daniel has two properties. His combined annual income is $520,000, and his combined debt service is $320,400. This results in a portfolio DSCR of approximately 1.62, which remains strong. His combined cash flow is approximately $199,600 per year.

After another two to three years, Daniel uses this increased cash flow and improved financial profile to refinance his first property. Due to appreciation and loan paydown, the property is now valued at $2,200,000, and his loan balance has decreased to $1,500,000. He refinances at a lower rate, reducing his monthly payment and freeing up an additional $1,000 per month in cash flow.

With increased cash flow and improved financials, Daniel is able to acquire a third property. This process continues, with each property contributing to the overall portfolio and strengthening his ability to qualify for additional financing.

After several years, Daniel owns a portfolio of four properties with a combined value of $8,000,000. His total debt service is approximately $650,000 per year, while his total net operating income is $1,100,000. This results in a portfolio DSCR of approximately 1.69 and annual cash flow of $450,000.

This example illustrates how scaling works through a combination of cash flow, reinvestment, refinancing, and strategic decision-making. Each property builds on the previous one, creating a compounding effect that accelerates growth. By maintaining strong financial metrics and managing risk effectively, Daniel is able to expand his portfolio while maintaining stability.

Through this process, SBA mortgage loans become more than just a financing tool—they become a foundation for long-term wealth creation.

Chapter 8

Exit Strategies and Long-Term Planning — How to Maximize Profit, Reduce Risk, and Control Your Financial Future with SBA Mortgage Loans

As you build experience with SBA mortgage loans, one of the most important concepts to master is the exit strategy. While many borrowers focus heavily on acquisition—getting approved, securing favorable terms, and closing the deal—far fewer give equal attention to how the loan and the asset will eventually be exited. However, the exit strategy is where profits are realized, risks are reduced, and long-term wealth is solidified. Without a clear exit plan, even a well-structured loan can lead to missed opportunities or unnecessary financial strain. This chapter is designed to help you think strategically about the end from the beginning, ensuring that every decision you make supports a profitable and controlled outcome.

An exit strategy is simply your plan for what you will do with the property or business over time. This could include selling the asset, refinancing into a better loan, holding for long-term cash flow, or transitioning into a different type of financing. Each of these paths has its own advantages, risks, and timing considerations. The key is to align your exit strategy with your overall financial goals and to structure your loan in a way that supports that strategy from the outset.

One of the most common exit strategies is refinancing. As your business grows, your financial profile improves, and market conditions change, you may have the opportunity to replace your SBA loan with a more favorable loan. This could involve lower interest rates, different loan structures, or transitioning into conventional financing that no longer requires SBA guarantees. Refinancing can reduce your monthly payments, improve cash flow, and free up capital for additional investments. However, it is important to understand the timing and costs associated with refinancing, including prepayment penalties and closing costs.

Another common exit strategy is selling the property or business. This approach allows you to realize the appreciation in value and capture the equity you have built over time. The success of this strategy depends on several factors, including market conditions, property performance, and timing. Selling at the right time can result in significant profits, while selling too early or during unfavorable market conditions can limit your returns. Planning your exit with an understanding of market cycles and your own financial position is essential for maximizing value. Long-term hold is another strategy that focuses on generating consistent cash flow and building wealth over time. In this approach, the property or business is retained, and the loan is managed in a way that supports stability and income generation. This often involves fixed-rate financing, conservative leverage, and a focus on operational efficiency. Over time, as the loan is paid down and the asset appreciates, your equity increases, creating a strong financial foundation.

Transition strategies are also important to consider. For example, you may start with an SBA loan to acquire a property and then transition to a conventional loan once your business stabilizes and your financial profile strengthens. This allows you to take advantage of SBA financing when it is most beneficial and then move into a different structure that may offer greater flexibility or lower costs. Planning for this transition from the beginning ensures that your loan terms do not create obstacles later.

Timing plays a critical role in all exit strategies. Market conditions, interest rates, and economic trends can all impact the optimal timing for refinancing or selling. While it is impossible to predict these factors with certainty, staying informed and monitoring trends can help you make more strategic decisions. Flexibility is also important, as your initial plan may need to be adjusted based on changing circumstances. Equity is a central component of exit strategy planning. As you make loan payments and as your property or business increases in value, you build equity. This equity represents your ownership stake and is a key source of profit when you sell or refinance. Understanding how your loan structure affects equity growth allows you to make decisions that enhance your long-term returns. For example, making additional principal payments can accelerate equity buildup, while maximizing cash flow may slow it down but provide other opportunities.

Tax considerations are another important factor in exit planning. The way you structure your ownership, manage depreciation, and execute your exit can all impact your tax liability. While this book does not provide tax advice, it is important to work with qualified professionals to ensure that your strategy is aligned with your tax objectives. Proper planning can help you retain more of your profits and enhance your overall financial outcome.

Risk reduction is also a key goal of exit strategies. By having a clear plan, you reduce uncertainty and improve your ability to respond to challenges. For example, knowing that you plan to refinance within a certain timeframe allows you to prepare your financials and monitor market conditions. Similarly, planning to sell at a specific stage of growth allows you to focus on maximizing value leading up to that point. Another important concept is optionality. A strong exit strategy provides you with multiple options rather than locking you into a single path. This flexibility allows you to adapt to changing conditions and choose the most advantageous course of action. For example, a well-structured loan with manageable prepayment terms allows you to either refinance or sell depending on market conditions. This level of flexibility is a significant advantage in dynamic markets.

As you integrate exit strategies into your overall approach to SBA mortgage financing, you begin to see the bigger picture. Each decision—from loan structure to cash flow management—contributes to your eventual outcome. By planning ahead and aligning your actions with your goals, you create a cohesive strategy that supports both immediate success and long-term wealth creation.

Ultimately, exit strategies are about control. They allow you to take charge of your financial future, rather than reacting to circumstances as they arise. By understanding your options, planning your path, and maintaining flexibility, you can maximize your returns, reduce risk, and achieve your long-term objectives.

As you complete this book, you will have a comprehensive understanding of SBA mortgage loans—from requirements and rates to structures, optimization, risk management, scaling, and exit strategies. With this knowledge, you are equipped to approach SBA financing not just as a borrower, but as a strategic operator capable of using financing as a powerful tool for growth and success.

Real-Life Math Example: Exit Strategy Through Refinancing and Sale for Maximum Profit

Let's walk through a detailed example to understand how exit strategies impact financial outcomes. Imagine a borrower named Sophia who purchases a commercial property for $2,400,000 using an SBA loan. She puts down 10 percent, or $240,000, resulting in a loan amount of $2,160,000 at an interest rate of 8.5 percent with a 25-year amortization.

Her monthly payment is approximately $16,700, resulting in an annual debt service of about $200,400. The property generates a net operating income of $320,000 per year, resulting in a DSCR of approximately 1.60. After debt service, Sophia has annual cash flow of approximately $119,600.

Sophia plans to hold the property for five years and then evaluate her exit options. During this time, she makes her regular loan payments, reducing the loan balance. After five years, her loan balance has decreased to approximately $1,950,000. At the same time, the property has appreciated to a value of $2,900,000 due to market growth and improved performance.

At this point, Sophia has built significant equity. The difference between the property value and the loan balance is approximately $950,000. She now considers two options: refinancing or selling.

If Sophia chooses to refinance, she may be able to secure a new loan at a lower interest rate, for example 7 percent. Assuming she refinances the remaining $1,950,000 over 25 years, her new monthly payment would be approximately $13,800, reducing her annual debt service to about $165,600. This increases her annual cash flow to approximately $154,400, providing an additional $34,800 per year.

Alternatively, Sophia could choose to sell the property. If she sells for $2,900,000 and pays off the remaining loan of $1,950,000, she is left with $950,000 before transaction costs. After accounting for selling expenses of approximately 6 percent, or $174,000, her net proceeds would be approximately $776,000. Compared to her initial investment of $240,000, this represents a profit of $536,000 over five years.

Now let's consider the impact of continued holding. If Sophia keeps the property after refinancing, her improved cash flow of $154,400 per year allows her to accumulate significant income over time. Over five additional years, this would result in approximately $772,000 in cash flow, not including further appreciation or equity growth.

This example highlights how different exit strategies can lead to different outcomes. Selling provides immediate profit and liquidity, while refinancing and holding provide ongoing cash flow and continued growth. The best choice depends on Sophia's goals, whether she prioritizes immediate returns or long-term income.

By planning her exit strategy from the beginning, Sophia is able to make informed decisions and maximize her financial outcome. This demonstrates the power of combining SBA mortgage financing with strategic planning to achieve long-term success.

Chapter 9

Building a Complete SBA Mortgage Strategy — Integrating Requirements, Rates, Structures, Risk, and Growth into One System

At this stage, you have developed a deep understanding of SBA mortgage loan requirements, interest rates, loan structures, optimization strategies, risk management, scaling, and exit planning. Each of these elements is powerful on its own, but the true advantage comes from integrating them into a single, cohesive strategy. This chapter is about bringing everything together—creating a system that allows you to approach SBA financing with clarity, confidence, and control. Instead of viewing each loan as an isolated transaction, you begin to see it as part of a larger framework designed to build long-term wealth and financial stability.

A complete SBA mortgage strategy starts with alignment. Every decision you make should align with your long-term goals. Are you focused on building a portfolio of income-producing properties? Are you aiming to scale a business through strategic acquisitions? Are you prioritizing cash flow, equity growth, or a combination of both? Without clear objectives, it is difficult to make effective decisions. Alignment ensures that your financing supports your strategy rather than working against it.

The next step is integrating borrower positioning with loan selection. As discussed in earlier chapters, your borrower profile plays a significant role in determining your loan terms. By strengthening your financials, improving your credit, maintaining liquidity, and demonstrating experience, you position yourself to qualify for better options. This, in turn, allows you to choose from a wider range of loan structures and negotiate more favorable terms. The stronger your foundation, the more flexibility you have in designing your strategy.

Interest rates and loan structures must then be evaluated within the context of your goals. A lower rate may reduce costs, but a more flexible structure may provide greater opportunities for growth. Similarly, a fixed-rate loan may offer stability, while a variable rate may provide short-term savings. The key is to evaluate these options not in isolation, but as part of a broader strategy. For example, if your goal is to scale quickly, prioritizing cash flow through longer amortization and lower initial payments may be more beneficial than minimizing total interest.

Risk management must also be integrated into your strategy.

Every decision carries some level of risk, and your goal is to manage that risk effectively. This involves maintaining strong cash flow, building reserves, diversifying your portfolio, and stress testing your loans. By proactively addressing potential risks, you create a more resilient financial position that can withstand changes in market conditions, interest rates, and business performance.

Scaling and growth are the natural progression of a well-executed strategy. As you complete successful transactions, you build experience, improve your financial profile, and create opportunities for additional investments. Each deal should strengthen your position and contribute to your ability to execute future deals. This requires discipline, patience, and a focus on long-term outcomes. Rapid growth without a strong foundation can lead to instability, while controlled, strategic growth can lead to sustainable success.

Exit planning is the final piece of the strategy. Every loan should have a clear path forward, whether that involves refinancing, selling, or holding long-term. By planning your exit from the beginning, you ensure that your decisions support your desired outcome. This includes understanding prepayment terms, monitoring market conditions, and aligning your loan structure with your exit timeline. A well-defined exit strategy provides clarity and reduces uncertainty. Another important aspect of a complete strategy is adaptability. Markets change, interest rates fluctuate, and business conditions evolve. A rigid strategy can become ineffective if it cannot adapt to new circumstances. By maintaining flexibility and continuously evaluating your position, you can adjust your approach as needed. This may involve refinancing, restructuring, or pursuing new opportunities that align with current conditions.

Data and analysis play a critical role in this process. By tracking your financial performance, monitoring key metrics, and evaluating each deal, you gain valuable insights that inform your decisions. This allows you to refine your strategy over time and improve your outcomes. Successful operators treat each transaction as a learning experience, using data to identify strengths and areas for improvement.

Another key component is consistency. Building a successful SBA mortgage strategy is not about one perfect deal—it is about executing a series of well-structured deals over time. Consistency in decision-making, risk management, and financial discipline creates momentum and leads to compounding results. Small improvements in each deal can lead to significant differences over time.

Relationships are also an integral part of a complete strategy. Working with experienced lenders, brokers, and advisors can provide valuable insights and opportunities. Strong relationships can lead to better terms, faster approvals, and access to deals that may not be available otherwise. Investing in these relationships is an important part of building a successful financing strategy.

As you integrate all of these elements, you begin to operate at a higher level. You are no longer reacting to opportunities—you are creating them. You are not just qualifying for loans—you are designing financing solutions that support your goals. This level of control and intentionality is what separates successful borrowers from true operators.

Ultimately, building a complete SBA mortgage strategy is about creating a system that works for you. It is about aligning your financing with your goals, managing risk, optimizing performance, and continuously improving your approach. By doing so, you transform SBA mortgage loans from a simple funding source into a powerful tool for long-term success.

As you move forward, remember that this strategy is not static. It will evolve as your goals, experience, and market conditions change. By staying informed, adaptable, and disciplined, you

can continue to refine your approach and achieve your objectives.

This chapter represents the culmination of everything you have learned in this book. By integrating requirements, rates, structures, optimization, risk management, scaling, and exit strategies into a cohesive system, you are equipped to approach SBA mortgage financing with confidence and clarity. The knowledge you have gained provides a foundation for building wealth, growing your business, and achieving financial independence.

Real-Life Math Example: Building a Multi-Deal SBA Strategy with Integrated Financial Planning

Let's walk through a comprehensive example to see how all elements come together in a complete SBA mortgage strategy. Imagine a borrower named Anthony who is building a portfolio of commercial properties using SBA loans.

Anthony begins with his first property, purchasing it for $2,000,000 with a 10 percent down payment of $200,000. The loan amount is $1,800,000 at an interest rate of 8.5 percent with a 25-year amortization. His monthly payment is approximately $14,400, resulting in annual debt service of $172,800.

The property generates a net operating income of $280,000 per year, resulting in a DSCR of approximately 1.62. After debt service, Anthony has $107,200 in annual cash flow. He uses this cash flow to build reserves and prepare for future investments. After two years, Anthony has accumulated $200,000 in additional capital and improved his financial profile. He uses this to acquire a second property for $2,500,000 with a similar structure. The loan amount is $2,250,000, with annual debt service of approximately $216,000. The property generates $350,000 in income, resulting in a DSCR of approximately 1.62.

Now Anthony has two properties with combined income of $630,000 and combined debt service of $388,800. His portfolio DSCR remains strong at approximately 1.62, and his total cash flow is $241,200 per year.

Anthony then focuses on optimization. He refinances his first property at a lower rate of 7.5 percent, reducing his annual debt service by $20,000. This increases his total cash flow and improves his ability to qualify for additional financing.

After another two years, Anthony acquires a third property for $3,000,000, using the same disciplined approach. His portfolio now includes three properties with a combined value of $7,500,000, total income of $1,050,000, and total debt service of approximately $650,000. His portfolio DSCR is approximately 1.62, and his annual cash flow is $400,000.

Anthony continues to manage risk by maintaining strong reserves and stress testing his portfolio. He ensures that his DSCR remains above 1.40 even under adverse scenarios. He also plans his exit strategy, identifying opportunities to refinance or sell properties based on market conditions.

After several years, Anthony's portfolio has grown to $10,000,000 in value, with significant equity and strong cash flow. By integrating all elements of SBA mortgage strategy—requirements, rates, structures, optimization, risk management, scaling, and exit planning—he has built a sustainable and profitable system.

This example demonstrates how a comprehensive approach to SBA financing can lead to long-term success. By treating each loan as part of a larger strategy, Anthony is able to maximize his opportunities and achieve his financial goals.

Chapter 10

Advanced SBA Commercial Mortgage Loan Structuring — Designing Complex Deals for Maximum Approval and Profitability

At the highest level of SBA mortgage financing, success is no longer determined by whether you can qualify, but by how well you can structure complex deals to maximize approval, optimize cash flow, and create long-term profitability. Advanced loan structuring is where strategy, creativity, and execution come together. It is the skill that allows experienced borrowers and operators to turn challenging transactions into successful opportunities. This chapter is designed to take everything you have learned throughout this book and elevate it into advanced structuring techniques that can be applied to more sophisticated deals.

Advanced structuring begins with understanding that no two deals are exactly the same. Each transaction has unique characteristics, including borrower profile, property type, business performance, and market conditions. This means that a one-size-fits-all approach is rarely effective. Instead, advanced structuring involves tailoring the loan to fit the specific needs of the deal while staying within SBA guidelines. This requires a deep understanding of how each component of the loan can be adjusted and how those adjustments impact the overall outcome.

One of the most important aspects of advanced structuring is layering multiple objectives into a single deal. For example, a borrower may want to acquire a business, purchase the associated real estate, and include working capital in the same transaction. An SBA 7(a) loan may allow for this level of flexibility, but the challenge lies in structuring the deal so that it meets underwriting requirements while still achieving the borrower's goals. This involves carefully balancing loan amounts, cash flow projections, and risk factors to create a structure that is both approvable and advantageous.

Cash flow engineering is a key component of advanced structuring. This involves designing the loan in a way that optimizes cash flow while maintaining compliance with lender requirements. Techniques may include adjusting amortization periods, incorporating interest-only phases, or structuring payments to align with business performance. The goal is to create a payment structure that supports the borrower's operations and allows for growth, rather than creating unnecessary financial pressure. Another important technique is combining different financing components to achieve a desired outcome. For example, a borrower may use an SBA loan for the majority of the financing while supplementing it with additional capital from other sources. This could include seller financing, equity contributions, or other forms of funding. By combining these elements, the borrower can reduce the loan amount, improve cash flow, and enhance the overall structure of the deal. This type of creative structuring requires careful planning and coordination but can significantly improve the outcome.

Risk mitigation is also a central focus in advanced structuring. Complex deals often involve higher levels of risk, whether due to larger loan amounts, multiple components, or less conventional scenarios. Managing this risk involves strengthening the borrower profile, ensuring strong cash flow coverage, and incorporating safeguards such as reserves and contingency plans. By addressing potential risks proactively, you increase the likelihood of approval and create a more stable financial position.

Another advanced concept is structuring for future flexibility. This involves designing the loan in a way that allows for refinancing, expansion, or other strategic moves down the line. For example, choosing a structure with manageable prepayment terms can provide the option to refinance when rates improve. Similarly, maintaining strong financial metrics can position you for additional financing in the future. Advanced structuring is not just about the current deal—it is about how that deal fits into your long-term strategy.

Negotiation becomes even more important at this level. Complex deals often require collaboration between multiple parties, including lenders, brokers, and sometimes sellers. Being able to communicate your strategy clearly and demonstrate the strength of your deal can help you secure better terms and overcome potential obstacles. This includes negotiating interest rates, fees, and structural components to create the most favorable outcome.

Documentation and presentation are also critical in advanced structuring. Complex deals require clear, organized, and well-supported documentation to gain lender confidence. This includes detailed financial statements, projections, and explanations of how the deal is structured. A strong presentation can make the difference between approval and rejection, especially in more complex scenarios.

Another key element is understanding how to use SBA guidelines to your advantage. While these guidelines establish certain limits, they also provide flexibility in many areas. By understanding these rules in detail, you can structure deals in a way that maximizes benefits while remaining compliant.

This includes knowing how to allocate funds, structure payments, and present financial information in a way that aligns with lender expectations.

As you develop your advanced structuring skills, you will begin to see opportunities where others see obstacles. Deals that may initially appear too complex or challenging can often be structured in a way that makes them viable. This ability to solve problems and create solutions is what defines high-level operators in the SBA financing space.

Ultimately, advanced structuring is about control and creativity. It is about taking the tools available within SBA mortgage financing and using them in a strategic and intentional way. By mastering this skill, you can unlock opportunities, improve outcomes, and build a more powerful and flexible financing strategy.

As you complete this book, you now have a comprehensive understanding of SBA mortgage financing at every level—from foundational concepts to advanced structuring techniques. With this knowledge, you are equipped to approach any SBA mortgage transaction with confidence, clarity, and strategic insight.

Real-Life Math Example: Structuring a Complex SBA Deal with Business Acquisition, Real Estate, and Working Capital

Let's walk through a detailed example to see how advanced structuring works in practice. Imagine a borrower named Marcus who is acquiring a business and its associated real estate. The total project cost is $4,000,000, which includes $3,200,000 for the business and property, and $800,000 for working capital and improvements.

Marcus plans to use an SBA 7(a) loan with a 10 percent down payment of $400,000, resulting in a loan amount of $3,600,000. The interest rate is 8.75 percent with a 25-year amortization. His monthly payment is approximately $28,500, resulting in annual debt service of $342,000.

The business generates a net operating income of $550,000 per year. This results in a DSCR of approximately 1.61 ($550,000 divided by $342,000), which is strong. However, Marcus wants to improve his cash flow and reduce risk.

To optimize the structure, Marcus negotiates a 2-year interest-only period. During this time, his monthly payment drops to approximately $26,250, reducing his annual debt service to $315,000. This increases his DSCR to approximately 1.75, providing stronger cash flow during the critical transition period. Marcus also incorporates seller financing of $200,000, reducing the SBA loan amount to $3,400,000. This lowers his monthly payment further and improves his overall financial position. The seller financing may be structured with favorable terms, such as deferred payments, which further enhance cash flow.

Now let's evaluate the long-term impact. With the reduced loan amount and optimized structure, Marcus saves approximately $200,000 in interest over the life of the loan. Additionally, the improved cash flow allows him to reinvest in the business, increasing its value and performance.

After three years, the business income increases to $650,000 per year due to operational improvements. Marcus then refinances the loan at a lower rate of 7.5 percent, reducing his monthly payment to approximately $25,000 and annual debt service to $300,000. This results in a DSCR of approximately 2.17, providing significant financial strength.

Through this process, Marcus transforms a complex transaction into a highly efficient and profitable deal. By combining multiple strategies—interest-only periods, seller financing, and refinancing—he is able to optimize his loan structure and achieve his goals.

This example demonstrates how advanced structuring can create value and improve outcomes. By understanding and applying these techniques, borrowers can take control of complex deals and turn them into powerful opportunities for growth and success.

Chapter 11

Mastering SBA Mortgage Loan Execution – From Application to Closing with Speed, Precision, and Control

Understanding SBA mortgage loan strategy is only part of the equation. The ability to execute—efficiently, accurately, and strategically—is what ultimately determines whether a deal closes successfully and on favorable terms. Many strong deals fail not because they are unqualified, but because they are poorly executed. Delays, missing documentation, miscommunication, and lack of preparation can all derail a transaction or weaken your negotiating position. This chapter is focused on mastering the execution process so you can move from application to closing with confidence, speed, and control.

Execution begins long before you submit a loan application. Preparation is the foundation of a smooth process. This includes organizing your financial documents, understanding your business and personal financials, and clearly defining the purpose of the loan. A well-prepared borrower not only speeds up the process but also builds credibility with lenders. When your documentation is complete, accurate, and easy to review, it reduces friction in underwriting and increases the likelihood of a favorable outcome.

The application phase is where your preparation is put into action. This involves submitting your financial information, business details, and supporting documentation to the lender. It is important to present a clear and consistent narrative that explains your deal, your experience, and your ability to repay the loan. Lenders are not just reviewing numbers—they are evaluating the overall story of the transaction. A strong, cohesive presentation can make a significant difference in how your application is perceived.

Once the application is submitted, the underwriting process begins. This is where the lender conducts a detailed analysis of your financials, the property, and the overall transaction. Underwriting is often the most complex and time-consuming part of the process. It involves verifying information, assessing risk, and ensuring that the loan meets both lender and SBA guidelines. During this phase, communication is critical. Responding quickly to requests for additional information and providing clear, accurate answers can help keep the process moving forward.

Conditions are a normal part of the underwriting process. These are requirements that must be satisfied before the loan can be approved and closed. Conditions may include additional documentation, clarifications, or adjustments to the loan structure. While some borrowers view conditions as obstacles, experienced operators see them as part of the process. The key is to address them efficiently and thoroughly. Delays in satisfying conditions can extend the timeline and create unnecessary complications.

Appraisal and property evaluation are also key components of the execution process. The lender will require an appraisal to confirm the value of the property and ensure that it supports the loan amount. Additionally, environmental assessments and inspections may be required to evaluate the condition and potential risks associated with the property. These steps are critical for both the lender and the borrower, as they provide a clearer understanding of the asset being financed.

Timing is one of the most important aspects of execution. SBA loans involve multiple steps and parties, and delays in any part of the process can impact the overall timeline. Managing this timeline requires coordination, communication, and attention to detail. Setting realistic expectations, tracking progress, and proactively addressing potential issues can help ensure that the deal moves forward smoothly. Another key element of execution is managing relationships. This includes working effectively with your lender, broker, attorney, and other professionals involved in the transaction. Clear communication and collaboration are essential for resolving issues and keeping the process on track. Building strong relationships can also lead to better outcomes, as experienced professionals can provide valuable insights and support.

Closing is the final stage of the execution process. This is where all conditions are satisfied, documents are finalized, and funds are disbursed. While this may seem like the end of the process, it is also a critical point where attention to detail is essential. Reviewing documents carefully, understanding your obligations, and ensuring that all terms are accurate can prevent issues down the line. A successful closing is the result of careful planning and execution throughout the entire process.

Post-closing management is often overlooked but equally important. Once the loan is closed, you must manage it effectively to ensure long-term success. This includes making timely payments, maintaining financial records, and monitoring performance. Strong post-closing management not only supports your current loan but also positions you for future opportunities.

Another important aspect of execution is efficiency. The faster you can move through the process, the more competitive you become as a borrower. Sellers and brokers often prefer buyers who can close quickly and reliably. By mastering execution, you can differentiate yourself and gain access to better opportunities.

Technology and systems can also play a role in improving execution. Using tools to organize documents, track progress, and communicate with your team can streamline the process and reduce errors. As your transactions become more complex, having efficient systems in place becomes increasingly important.

As you develop your execution skills, you will begin to see patterns and opportunities for improvement. Each transaction provides valuable experience that can be applied to future deals. By continuously refining your approach, you can become more efficient, reduce risk, and improve outcomes.

Ultimately, mastering execution is about discipline and attention to detail. It is about taking a proactive approach, staying organized, and maintaining clear communication throughout the process. By doing so, you can ensure that your deals close successfully and that your financing supports your long-term goals.

This chapter represents the final step in your journey through SBA mortgage loan mastery. By combining strong strategy with effective execution, you are equipped to approach any transaction with confidence and control. The knowledge and skills you have developed throughout this book provide a foundation for building a successful and sustainable financing strategy.

Real-Life Math Example: Timeline, Costs, and Financial Impact of Efficient vs Delayed SBA Loan Execution

Let's walk through a detailed example to understand how execution impacts financial outcomes. Imagine a borrower named Kevin who is purchasing a commercial property for $2,200,000. He is using an SBA loan with a 10 percent down payment of $220,000, resulting in a loan amount of $1,980,000 at an interest rate of 8.5 percent.

Kevin's monthly payment is approximately $15,400, resulting in annual debt service of $184,800. The property generates a net operating income of $290,000 per year, resulting in a DSCR of approximately 1.57.

Now let's compare two scenarios: efficient execution and delayed execution.

In the efficient execution scenario, Kevin completes his documentation quickly, responds to lender requests promptly, and closes the loan in 60 days. During this time, he incurs minimal additional costs, such as interest rate lock fees and minor holding costs. He begins generating income from the property immediately after closing, allowing him to capture the full annual cash flow of approximately $105,200 after debt service.

In the delayed execution scenario, Kevin is unprepared and takes longer to provide documentation. The process extends to 120 days. During this additional 60-day period, he incurs holding costs, including rent for his current location, lost income opportunities, and potential increases in interest rates.

Let's quantify these costs. Suppose Kevin incurs $10,000 per month in holding costs during the delay. Over 60 days, this amounts to $20,000. Additionally, if interest rates increase by 0.5 percent during this period, his monthly payment rises to approximately $16,000, increasing his annual debt service to $192,000.

With the higher payment, Kevin's DSCR decreases to approximately 1.51 ($290,000 divided by $192,000), and his annual cash flow decreases to $98,000. Over time, this difference compounds, reducing his overall profitability.

Now consider the opportunity cost. By delaying the closing, Kevin also loses two months of income from the property.

With a monthly net income of approximately $8,750 ($105,200 divided by 12), this results in an additional loss of $17,500.

In total, the delayed execution costs Kevin approximately $37,500 in direct and opportunity costs, plus higher ongoing payments due to the increased interest rate. Over the life of the loan, the higher rate could result in tens of thousands of dollars in additional interest.

This example demonstrates how execution directly impacts financial outcomes. Efficient execution not only reduces costs but also improves cash flow and profitability. By contrast, delays can create significant financial disadvantages.

By mastering the execution process, borrowers can protect their deals, reduce costs, and maximize their financial success.

Chapter 12

Long-Term Wealth Creation with SBA Mortgage Loans — Building a Financial Legacy Through Strategic Financing

At the highest level, SBA mortgage financing is not just about acquiring property or securing a loan—it is about creating long-term wealth, financial independence, and a lasting legacy. Everything you have learned throughout this series—requirements, rates, structures, optimization, risk management, scaling, execution, and exit strategies—leads to this final outcome. The true power of SBA mortgage loans lies in their ability to serve as a foundation for building assets that generate income, appreciate in value, and create opportunities for future generations. This chapter is designed to help you understand how to use SBA financing as a long-term wealth-building system rather than a series of isolated transactions.

Wealth creation begins with ownership. When you use SBA financing to acquire commercial real estate or businesses, you are gaining control over income-producing assets. Unlike renting or leasing, ownership allows you to benefit from both cash flow and appreciation. Each payment you make reduces your loan balance, increasing your equity. Over time, this equity becomes a powerful financial resource that can be leveraged for additional investments or realized through sale or refinancing.

One of the most important concepts in long-term wealth creation is compounding. As you reinvest your cash flow into additional assets, your income grows, creating a cycle of expansion. Each new acquisition contributes to your overall portfolio, increasing both your income and your equity. Over time, this compounding effect can lead to exponential growth. The key is consistency—continuing to acquire, manage, and optimize assets over time.

Cash flow plays a central role in this process. Positive cash flow provides the capital needed to reinvest and expand. It also creates financial stability, allowing you to manage your obligations and take advantage of opportunities. Structuring your SBA loans to maximize cash flow can accelerate your ability to scale and build wealth. This may involve choosing longer amortization periods, optimizing interest rates, and managing expenses effectively.

Equity growth is another critical component. As your properties appreciate and your loan balances decrease, your equity increases. This equity represents your ownership stake and can be used to support future investments. For example, you may be able to refinance a property to access its equity and use those funds as a down payment for another acquisition. This allows you to leverage your existing assets to continue growing your portfolio.

Leverage is one of the most powerful tools in real estate and business financing. SBA loans allow you to acquire assets with relatively low down payments, enabling you to control larger investments with less capital. When used responsibly, leverage can amplify your returns and accelerate wealth creation. However, it must be managed carefully to avoid excessive risk. Maintaining strong cash flow and reserves is essential for balancing leverage and stability.

Another important aspect of long-term wealth creation is diversification. Building a portfolio that includes multiple properties or businesses can reduce risk and enhance stability. Different assets may perform differently under various market conditions, providing a buffer against volatility. Diversification also creates multiple income streams, which can strengthen your overall financial position.

Time is one of the most powerful factors in wealth creation. The longer you hold and manage your assets effectively, the greater the potential for growth. Appreciation, loan paydown, and reinvestment all compound over time, leading to significant increases in value. Patience and discipline are essential for maximizing these benefits.

Tax efficiency is also an important consideration. While specific strategies should be discussed with qualified professionals, understanding how ownership, depreciation, and financing impact your tax position can enhance your overall returns. Proper planning can help you retain more of your income and reinvest it into your portfolio.

Another key concept is financial independence. As your portfolio grows and your cash flow increases, you may reach a point where your passive income covers your living expenses. This provides freedom and flexibility, allowing you to focus on your goals and priorities. SBA financing can play a significant role in achieving this outcome by enabling you to acquire income-producing assets.

Legacy building is the final stage of wealth creation. The assets you acquire and the systems you build can be passed on to future generations, creating long-term benefits for your family or community. This may involve structuring ownership, creating succession plans, and ensuring that your portfolio is managed effectively over time. By thinking beyond your own financial goals, you can create a lasting impact.

As you reflect on everything you have learned in this series, it becomes clear that SBA mortgage financing is more than just a tool—it is a system. When used strategically, it can provide a pathway to financial growth, stability, and independence. Each decision you make contributes to this system, shaping your financial future.

The journey does not end with a single loan or property. It is an ongoing process of learning, adapting, and improving. By staying informed, maintaining discipline, and focusing on your long-term goals, you can continue to build and refine your strategy.

Ultimately, long-term wealth creation is about consistency, strategy, and execution. It is about making informed decisions, managing risk, and taking advantage of opportunities. With the knowledge you have gained, you are equipped to approach SBA mortgage financing with a clear vision and a strong foundation.

This chapter represents the culmination of your journey through the SBA Commercial Mortgage Loan Mastery Series. By applying these principles, you can transform financing into a powerful tool for building wealth, achieving financial independence, and creating a lasting legacy.

Real-Life Math Example: Building Long-Term Wealth Through SBA Financing and Compounding Growth

Let's walk through a comprehensive example to understand how SBA financing can be used to build long-term wealth. Imagine a borrower named Olivia who begins her journey by purchasing a commercial property for $1,500,000 using an SBA loan. She puts down 10 percent, or $150,000, resulting in a loan amount of $1,350,000 at an interest rate of 8.5 percent with a 25-year amortization.

Her monthly payment is approximately $10,400, resulting in annual debt service of $124,800. The property generates a net operating income of $200,000 per year, resulting in a DSCR of approximately 1.60. After debt service, Olivia has annual cash flow of approximately $75,200.

Instead of spending this cash flow, Olivia reinvests it. After two years, she has accumulated $150,000 in additional capital. Combined with some appreciation in the property value, she is able to acquire a second property for $1,800,000 with a similar structure.

The second property generates $240,000 in income, with annual debt service of approximately $150,000, resulting in additional cash flow of $90,000. Now Olivia's total annual cash flow is approximately $165,200.

Over time, Olivia continues this process, reinvesting her cash flow and acquiring additional properties. After five years, she owns three properties with a combined value of approximately $5,500,000. Her total annual income is $680,000, and her total debt service is $420,000, resulting in annual cash flow of $260,000.

As her portfolio grows, Olivia benefits from appreciation and loan paydown. After ten years, her properties have increased in value to $7,500,000, and her loan balances have decreased significantly. Her equity has grown to over $3,000,000.

At this point, Olivia has multiple options. She can continue to hold her properties and generate strong cash flow, refinance to access her equity, or sell some assets to realize profits. Her annual cash flow has grown to over $400,000, providing financial independence.

This example demonstrates how SBA financing can be used to create a compounding growth effect. By reinvesting cash flow, managing loans effectively, and making strategic decisions, Olivia is able to build significant wealth over time.

Through consistency and discipline, SBA mortgage loans become a powerful tool for long-term financial success, enabling borrowers to move from a single property to a diversified portfolio and ultimately achieve their financial goals.

Chapter 13

Creating a Repeatable SBA Mortgage System — From One Deal to a Predictable Wealth Machine

At the highest level of mastery, success with SBA mortgage loans is no longer about individual deals—it is about building a repeatable system. A system that consistently identifies opportunities, secures financing, executes efficiently, manages assets, and reinvests profits to generate continuous growth. This is where you transition from being a borrower to becoming an operator. A borrower completes transactions. An operator builds a machine. This chapter is focused on helping you design that machine—a predictable, scalable system that turns SBA mortgage financing into a long-term wealth engine.

The first step in building a repeatable system is standardization. Every successful system relies on repeatable processes. Instead of approaching each deal from scratch, you create a framework that can be applied consistently. This includes how you evaluate deals, how you prepare documentation, how you communicate with lenders, and how you structure your loans. By standardizing these processes, you reduce errors, increase efficiency, and improve outcomes.

Over time, this consistency becomes one of your greatest advantages.

Deal sourcing is the starting point of your system. Without a steady flow of opportunities, even the best strategy cannot be executed. This involves building relationships with brokers, agents, lenders, and other professionals who can provide access to deals. It also includes developing your own methods for identifying opportunities, whether through direct outreach, marketing, or analyzing market trends. A strong deal pipeline ensures that you always have options and can select the best opportunities rather than settling for what is available.

Once a deal is identified, the next step is analysis. This is where you evaluate whether the opportunity aligns with your strategy. Key factors include cash flow, risk, market conditions, and long-term potential. By using consistent criteria and financial models, you can quickly determine whether a deal meets your standards. This allows you to move efficiently and confidently, focusing your time and resources on the most promising opportunities.

Financing is the core of your system, and this is where your expertise in SBA mortgage loans becomes critical. By understanding requirements, rates, and structures, you can design financing solutions that support your goals. This includes selecting the right loan program, negotiating favorable terms, and structuring the loan to optimize cash flow and flexibility. Over time, as you build relationships with lenders and demonstrate a track record of success, your ability to secure financing improves, further strengthening your system.

Execution is the engine that drives your system. Efficient execution ensures that deals move from concept to closing without unnecessary delays or complications. This requires organization, communication, and attention to detail. By refining your execution process and learning from each transaction, you can continuously improve your efficiency and reliability. This not only enhances your own performance but also makes you a more attractive partner to lenders and sellers.

Asset management is where your system begins to generate results. Once a deal is closed, your focus shifts to managing the property or business effectively. This includes optimizing operations, controlling expenses, and maximizing income. Strong asset management ensures that your investments perform as expected and continue to generate positive cash flow. It also provides the foundation for future growth, as well-performing assets strengthen your financial profile.

Reinvestment is the key to scaling your system. The cash flow and equity generated from your existing assets can be used to acquire additional properties or businesses. This creates a cycle of growth, where each new acquisition builds on the previous ones. By consistently reinvesting your profits, you can accelerate your expansion and increase your overall wealth.

Automation and delegation are important as your system grows. While you may handle many aspects of the process initially, scaling requires leveraging other people and tools. This may include hiring team members, working with property managers, or using technology to streamline processes. By delegating tasks and automating workflows, you can focus on higher-level strategy and continue to grow your system.

Another critical component of a repeatable system is performance tracking. By monitoring key metrics such as cash flow, debt service coverage, and return on investment, you can evaluate the effectiveness of your strategy. This data allows you to identify areas for improvement and make informed decisions. Over time, this continuous feedback loop helps you refine your system and enhance your results.

Risk management must also be integrated into your system. As you scale, your exposure to risk increases, making it even more important to maintain strong financial discipline. This includes maintaining reserves, diversifying your portfolio, and stress testing your investments. By managing risk effectively, you protect your system and ensure its long-term sustainability. Consistency is the defining characteristic of a successful system. It is not about occasional success, but about repeated success over time. This requires discipline, patience, and a commitment to your strategy. By following your processes and maintaining focus, you can create a system that delivers reliable results.

As your system matures, you begin to experience the benefits of compounding. Each deal contributes to your overall growth, and the combined effect becomes increasingly powerful. What started as a single transaction evolves into a portfolio of assets that generate significant income and equity.

Ultimately, building a repeatable SBA mortgage system is about creating leverage. It is about using your knowledge, processes, and resources to achieve results that go beyond what is possible with individual efforts. By designing and refining your system, you can transform SBA financing into a predictable and scalable wealth machine.

This chapter represents the final evolution of your journey. You have moved from understanding individual components to integrating them into a comprehensive strategy, and now to building a system that can operate and grow over time. With this system in place, you are no longer limited by individual deals—you are positioned to create ongoing success.

Real-Life Math Example: Building a Repeatable SBA System That Generates $1M+ Annual Cash Flow

Let's walk through a detailed example to understand how a repeatable SBA system can create significant financial results. Imagine a borrower named Victor who begins with a single SBA-financed property and builds a system over time.

Victor starts by purchasing a property for $2,000,000 with a 10 percent down payment of $200,000. The loan amount is $1,800,000 at an interest rate of 8.5 percent with a 25-year amortization. His annual debt service is approximately $172,800, and the property generates $300,000 in net operating income. This results in annual cash flow of $127,200.

Victor reinvests this cash flow and, after two years, accumulates $250,000 in capital. He uses this to acquire a second property for $2,500,000, generating $350,000 in income with annual debt service of $216,000. This adds $134,000 in cash flow.

Now Victor's total annual cash flow is approximately $261,200. He continues this process, acquiring a third property after another two years. This property generates $400,000 in income with $260,000 in debt service, adding $140,000 in cash flow.

At this point, Victor owns three properties with total annual cash flow of approximately $401,200. He refines his system, improving efficiency and building relationships with lenders, allowing him to acquire properties more quickly.

Over the next five years, Victor acquires three additional properties, each generating approximately $150,000 in annual cash flow. This adds $450,000 to his total, bringing his annual cash flow to approximately $851,200.

Victor also optimizes his portfolio by refinancing some properties at lower rates, increasing cash flow by an additional $150,000 per year. This brings his total annual cash flow to over $1,000,000.

His portfolio now consists of six properties with a combined value of over $15,000,000. His total net operating income is approximately $2,200,000, and his total debt service is approximately $1,200,000, resulting in strong cash flow and a portfolio DSCR of approximately 1.83.

This example demonstrates how a repeatable system can generate significant results over time. By consistently sourcing deals, structuring financing, executing efficiently, managing assets, and reinvesting profits, Victor is able to build a scalable and predictable wealth machine.

Through discipline, strategy, and execution, SBA mortgage loans become more than a financing tool—they become the foundation of a system that creates long-term financial success.

Chapter 14

Leveraging SBA Mortgage Loans for Market Cycles — How to Win in Any Economy

One of the most overlooked advantages of SBA mortgage financing is its ability to be used strategically across different market cycles. Many borrowers only think about financing in the context of the current moment—what rates are today, what the market looks like today, and whether the deal works today. However, experienced operators think in cycles. They understand that markets move, interest rates fluctuate, and opportunities shift over time. The key to long-term success is not predicting the market perfectly, but positioning yourself to win in any environment. This chapter is focused on helping you understand market cycles and how to use SBA mortgage loans to your advantage in each phase.

Every market goes through cycles: expansion, peak, contraction, and recovery. During expansion, property values rise, businesses grow, and financing is relatively accessible. During peak periods, valuations may become inflated, and competition increases. In contraction phases, values may decline, and financing becomes more conservative. Recovery periods present new opportunities as the market stabilizes and begins to grow again. Understanding these phases allows you to adjust your strategy and make more informed decisions.

During expansion phases, SBA loans can be used to acquire assets that generate strong cash flow and have growth potential. The key during this phase is discipline. It can be tempting to overpay or take on excessive risk when the market is strong, but maintaining conservative underwriting standards ensures that your deals remain viable even if conditions change. Structuring your loans with manageable payments and maintaining reserves provides a buffer against future downturns.

At market peaks, caution becomes even more important. Prices may be high, and competition can lead to aggressive bidding. During this phase, the focus should shift toward protecting downside risk. This may involve being more selective with deals, negotiating stronger terms, and ensuring that your financing structure can withstand potential declines in value or income. Fixed-rate financing can be particularly valuable during this phase, as it protects against rising interest rates.

During contraction phases, opportunities begin to emerge. While some borrowers may pull back due to uncertainty, experienced operators recognize that this is often the best time to acquire assets at favorable prices. SBA financing can still be used effectively during these periods, particularly for strong borrowers with solid financial profiles. The key is to focus on deals with strong fundamentals—properties and businesses that can perform even in challenging conditions.

Recovery phases are where momentum begins to build again. As the market stabilizes, values start to rise, and opportunities become more abundant. Borrowers who positioned themselves during the contraction phase are often in a strong position to benefit from this growth. SBA loans can be used to expand portfolios, refinance existing loans, and capitalize on improving conditions.

Interest rates are closely tied to market cycles and play a significant role in your strategy. During periods of low rates, locking in fixed-rate financing can provide long-term advantages. During periods of rising rates, focusing on cash flow and maintaining flexibility becomes more important. Understanding how rates interact with market conditions allows you to make more strategic decisions about when to borrow and how to structure your loans.

Another important concept is timing your refinancing strategy. Market cycles often create opportunities to refinance at more favorable terms. For example, during a recovery phase, as rates stabilize or decline, refinancing can reduce your payments and improve cash flow. Planning for these opportunities allows you to maximize the benefits of changing market conditions.

Cash flow remains the most important factor across all market cycles. Regardless of whether the market is expanding or contracting, strong cash flow provides stability and flexibility. It allows you to weather downturns, take advantage of opportunities, and continue building your portfolio. Structuring your SBA loans to prioritize cash flow ensures that your strategy remains resilient.

Reserves and liquidity are also critical in navigating market cycles. Having sufficient reserves allows you to manage unexpected challenges and avoid being forced to sell assets at unfavorable times. This financial cushion provides the flexibility to hold through downturns and benefit from eventual recoveries.

Diversification is another key strategy for managing market cycles. By spreading your investments across different property types, locations, or business sectors, you reduce your exposure to any single market. This can enhance stability and improve your overall resilience.

Mindset plays a significant role in how you navigate market cycles. Fear and uncertainty can lead to missed opportunities, while overconfidence can lead to excessive risk. Maintaining a disciplined, long-term perspective allows you to make rational decisions regardless of market conditions. By focusing on fundamentals and sticking to your strategy, you can navigate cycles effectively.

As you integrate market cycle awareness into your SBA mortgage strategy, you begin to operate at a higher level. You are no longer reacting to the market—you are positioning yourself within it. This allows you to take advantage of opportunities, manage risk, and build wealth consistently over time.

Ultimately, the goal is not to time the market perfectly, but to build a strategy that works in any environment. By combining strong fundamentals, disciplined decision-making, and strategic use of SBA financing, you can create a system that thrives across cycles.

Real-Life Math Example: Using SBA Loans to Profit Through Market Cycles

Let's walk through a detailed example to see how market cycles impact SBA financing decisions. Imagine a borrower named Luis who purchases a commercial property during an expansion phase for $2,500,000. He uses an SBA loan with a 10 percent down payment of $250,000, resulting in a loan amount of $2,250,000 at an interest rate of 7.5 percent. His annual debt service is approximately $200,000, and the property generates $320,000 in net operating income, resulting in a DSCR of 1.60 and cash flow of $120,000.

As the market reaches its peak, property values increase to $2,800,000. Luis considers selling but decides to hold, focusing on cash flow and long-term growth. He maintains strong reserves and avoids taking on additional high-risk debt.

During a contraction phase, property values decline by 10 percent, bringing the value to approximately $2,520,000. While some investors face challenges, Luis's strong cash flow and conservative structure allow him to continue operating without issues. His DSCR remains above 1.50, providing stability.

At this point, Luis identifies a new opportunity—a distressed property priced at $2,000,000 that was previously valued at $2,400,000. He uses SBA financing again, with a loan amount of $1,800,000 and annual debt service of $170,000. The property generates $280,000 in income, resulting in cash flow of $110,000.

As the market enters recovery, both properties increase in value. The first property rises to $3,000,000, and the second to $2,400,000. Luis's combined portfolio value is now $5,400,000. He then refinances his first property at a lower rate of 6.5 percent, reducing his annual debt service by $30,000 and increasing cash flow. His total annual cash flow across both properties increases to approximately $260,000.

Over time, Luis continues to apply this strategy, acquiring properties during downturns and optimizing his portfolio during recoveries. By understanding and leveraging market cycles, he is able to build a portfolio that grows in both value and income.

This example demonstrates how SBA financing can be used strategically across different market conditions. By maintaining discipline, focusing on cash flow, and positioning himself effectively, Luis is able to navigate cycles and create long-term success.

Chapter 15

The SBA Mortgage Wealth Blueprint – Turning Knowledge into Lifelong Financial Freedom

At this point in your journey, you have developed a complete understanding of SBA mortgage financing—from foundational requirements and rate structures to advanced deal structuring, execution, scaling, and system-building. Now it is time to bring everything together into a single, actionable blueprint that you can follow for the rest of your financial life. This chapter is not about learning something new—it is about applying everything you already know in a disciplined, repeatable way that produces consistent results. This is your SBA Mortgage Wealth Blueprint.

The blueprint begins with clarity of vision. Without a clear destination, even the best strategy loses direction. You must define what success looks like for you. Is it financial independence through passive income? Is it building a multi-million-dollar portfolio of commercial real estate? Is it creating a business empire that generates long-term cash flow? Your vision determines your strategy, your pace, and your decisions. Every loan, every property, and every financial move should align with this vision. The next step is establishing your financial foundation. This includes your credit profile, liquidity, income stability, and financial discipline. These elements determine your ability to access financing and influence the terms you receive. Strengthening your foundation is one of the highest-return activities you can focus on. Improving your credit, increasing your reserves, and maintaining consistent financial performance all contribute to better opportunities and lower costs over time.

Once your foundation is in place, the blueprint moves into acquisition. This is where you begin identifying and securing opportunities that align with your strategy. The key is to focus on quality over quantity. Not every deal is worth pursuing. By applying consistent criteria—strong cash flow, manageable risk, and long-term potential—you ensure that each acquisition contributes positively to your overall system. This disciplined approach prevents over-leveraging and builds a portfolio that can withstand challenges.

Financing is the engine that powers your blueprint. By mastering SBA mortgage loans, you have the ability to acquire assets with relatively low capital while maintaining control and flexibility. The key is to structure each loan in a way that supports your strategy. This includes optimizing rates, choosing appropriate amortization, managing prepayment terms, and ensuring strong cash flow. Each loan should be viewed not just as a transaction, but as a strategic move within your larger plan.

Execution is what turns your blueprint into reality. Efficient, organized, and disciplined execution ensures that your deals close smoothly and on time. This includes preparing documentation, managing timelines, and communicating effectively with all parties involved. Strong execution not only improves outcomes but also enhances your reputation, making it easier to secure future opportunities.

Once an asset is acquired, management becomes the focus. Effective asset management ensures that your investments perform as expected and continue to generate positive cash flow. This includes optimizing operations, controlling expenses, and maintaining the property or business. Strong management is essential for sustaining performance and building long-term value.

Reinvestment is the mechanism that drives growth. The cash flow and equity generated from your assets should be reinvested into new opportunities. This creates a cycle of expansion, where each deal builds on the previous ones. Over time, this cycle leads to compounding growth, significantly increasing your income and net worth.

Risk management is integrated throughout the blueprint. Every decision you make should consider potential risks and include safeguards to mitigate them. This includes maintaining reserves, stress testing your portfolio, and avoiding excessive leverage. By managing risk effectively, you protect your system and ensure its long-term sustainability.

Scaling is the natural progression of a well-executed blueprint. As your portfolio grows, your experience, financial strength, and access to opportunities increase. This allows you to move more efficiently and pursue larger or more complex deals. However, scaling must be done strategically to maintain balance and stability.

Exit strategies are the final component of the blueprint. Each asset should have a clear path forward, whether that involves refinancing, selling, or holding long-term. By planning your exits, you ensure that you maximize value and maintain control over your financial outcomes. This also provides flexibility to adapt to changing market conditions.

Another critical aspect of the blueprint is discipline. Success in SBA mortgage financing is not about making one great decision—it is about making consistently good decisions over time. This requires patience, focus, and a commitment to your strategy. By maintaining discipline, you avoid common pitfalls and stay aligned with your long-term goals. As your blueprint evolves, it becomes a system that operates with increasing efficiency. Each component—acquisition, financing, execution, management, reinvestment, and scaling—works together to create a cycle of growth. This system becomes more powerful over time, as experience and resources compound.

The ultimate goal of the SBA Mortgage Wealth Blueprint is financial freedom. This is the point where your income from your assets exceeds your expenses, allowing you to live without financial stress. Beyond that, it is about creating options—having the ability to choose how you spend your time, pursue your interests, and build a legacy.

Legacy is the final stage of the blueprint. The assets and systems you create can be passed on to future generations, providing long-term benefits beyond your own lifetime. This may involve structuring ownership, planning for succession, and ensuring that your system can continue to operate effectively.

As you reflect on everything you have learned, it becomes clear that SBA mortgage financing is more than just a tool—it is a pathway. A pathway to building assets, generating income, and achieving financial independence. By following this blueprint, you can turn knowledge into action and action into results.

This chapter represents the culmination of your journey. You now have the knowledge, the strategy, and the framework to succeed. The next step is execution—taking what you have learned and applying it consistently over time.

Real-Life Math Example: Following the SBA Mortgage Wealth Blueprint to Achieve Financial Freedom

Let's walk through a detailed example to see how the SBA Mortgage Wealth Blueprint works in practice. Imagine a borrower named Rachel who starts with a clear goal: to generate $500,000 per year in passive income within 10 years.

Rachel begins with her first acquisition, purchasing a commercial property for $1,800,000 with a 10 percent down payment of $180,000. Her loan amount is $1,620,000 at an interest rate of 8.5 percent with a 25-year amortization. Her annual debt service is approximately $150,000, and the property generates $250,000 in net operating income, resulting in $100,000 in annual cash flow.

Rachel reinvests this cash flow and, after two years, accumulates $200,000. She uses this to acquire a second property for $2,200,000, generating $300,000 in income with $180,000 in debt service, resulting in $120,000 in cash flow.

Now Rachel's total annual cash flow is $220,000. She continues this process, acquiring a third property after another two years. This property generates $350,000 in income with $220,000 in debt service, adding $130,000 in cash flow. At this point, Rachel's total annual cash flow is $350,000. She continues to reinvest and optimize her portfolio, including refinancing properties to reduce interest rates and improve cash flow.

By year eight, Rachel owns four properties with total annual cash flow of approximately $480,000. Through continued optimization and growth, she acquires a fifth property, adding another $120,000 in cash flow.

Now Rachel's total annual cash flow exceeds $600,000, surpassing her original goal of $500,000. Her portfolio is valued at over $10,000,000, with significant equity and strong financial stability.

This example demonstrates how following a structured blueprint can lead to financial freedom. By consistently applying the principles of acquisition, financing, execution, management, and reinvestment, Rachel is able to achieve her goals and build long-term wealth.

Through discipline and strategy, SBA mortgage loans become a powerful tool for transforming financial goals into reality.

Closing Thoughts

From Knowledge to Action — Your Next Chapter Begins Now

You have reached the end of this journey, but in many ways, this is where everything truly begins. Throughout this series, you have explored the full spectrum of SBA mortgage financing—from understanding the fundamentals to mastering advanced strategies, from structuring deals to building systems, from managing risk to creating long-term wealth. What started as information has now become a framework, a blueprint, and ultimately a pathway forward. The knowledge you now hold is powerful, but its true value will only be realized through action.

At the beginning of this journey, SBA mortgage loans may have seemed complex, even overwhelming. There were requirements to understand, rates to evaluate, structures to consider, and processes to navigate. But as you progressed, those complexities began to transform into clarity. You started to see patterns, connections, and opportunities. What once felt like a barrier has now become a tool—a tool that you can use to build, grow, and expand your financial future.

One of the most important realizations you should take from this series is that financing is not just about borrowing money. It is about positioning yourself. It is about creating opportunities. It is about using leverage in a strategic and disciplined way to achieve outcomes that would otherwise be out of reach. When you understand how to use financing effectively, you move from reacting to circumstances to shaping them.

Another key takeaway is that success in SBA mortgage financing is not determined by a single decision or a single deal. It is the result of consistent, disciplined action over time. Each deal you evaluate, each loan you structure, each property you manage—all of these contribute to your overall trajectory. Small improvements in each step can lead to significant differences over time. This is the power of compounding, not just in financial terms, but in knowledge, experience, and execution.

You have also learned that strategy matters. Not every deal is the right deal. Not every loan structure is optimal. Not every opportunity aligns with your goals. The ability to evaluate, compare, and choose strategically is what separates successful operators from average participants. By applying the frameworks and principles you have learned, you can approach each opportunity with clarity and confidence.

Risk is an inevitable part of any financial journey, but it does not have to be a barrier. When you understand risk, measure it, and manage it effectively, it becomes something you can control rather than something that controls you. Maintaining strong cash flow, building reserves, diversifying your portfolio, and stress testing your investments are all ways to create resilience. This resilience allows you to navigate challenges and continue moving forward.

Execution is where everything comes together. Ideas, strategies, and plans only become real through action. The ability to move efficiently, communicate clearly, and manage the details of each transaction is what turns opportunities into results. By refining your execution process, you not only improve your outcomes but also build a reputation that opens doors to future opportunities.

As you think about scaling and growth, remember that it is not about moving as fast as possible—it is about moving intelligently. Sustainable growth is built on a strong foundation. Each step should reinforce your position, not weaken it. By maintaining discipline and focusing on long-term goals, you can create a trajectory that leads to lasting success.

The concept of a system is one of the most powerful ideas you have encountered. When you move from individual deals to a repeatable system, everything changes. Your efforts become more efficient, your results become more predictable, and your opportunities expand. This system becomes your engine—driving growth, generating income, and creating momentum.

Long-term wealth is not built overnight. It is built through patience, consistency, and strategic decision-making. It is the result of showing up, evaluating opportunities, making informed decisions, and following through. Over time, these actions compound, creating results that may have once seemed out of reach.

Financial freedom is not just about numbers—it is about options. It is about having the ability to choose how you spend your time, where you focus your energy, and what you prioritize in your life. The strategies you have learned are tools to help you move toward that freedom. How you use them will determine the outcome.

Legacy is the final dimension of this journey. The assets you build, the systems you create, and the knowledge you apply can extend beyond your own lifetime. By thinking long-term and planning intentionally, you can create something that benefits not only you but also those who come after you. This is where your efforts take on a deeper meaning.

As you move forward, it is important to remember that

learning does not stop here. The market will change, new opportunities will emerge, and your own goals may evolve. Staying informed, adaptable, and open to growth will allow you to continue refining your approach. Each experience will add to your knowledge and strengthen your strategy.

There will be challenges along the way. Deals that do not work out, unexpected obstacles, and moments of uncertainty. These are all part of the process. What matters is how you respond. By applying the principles you have learned, you can navigate these challenges and continue moving forward.

Confidence comes from preparation and experience. The more you apply what you have learned, the more confident you will become. Each successful transaction reinforces your understanding and builds momentum. Over time, what once felt complex becomes second nature.

Discipline is your greatest ally. It keeps you focused, prevents impulsive decisions, and ensures that you stay aligned with your goals. By maintaining discipline, you create consistency, and consistency leads to results.

Opportunity is everywhere, but it is not always obvious. The ability to recognize and act on opportunities is what sets successful individuals apart. With the knowledge you now have, you are better equipped to identify these opportunities and take advantage of them.

Action is the bridge between knowledge and results. Without action, even the best strategies remain theoretical. The next step is to take what you have learned and apply it. Start with one deal, one decision, one step forward. Momentum builds from there.

As you close this book, you are not at the end—you are at the beginning of a new phase. A phase where you take control of your financial future, where you apply strategy with intention, and where you build something meaningful over time.

The tools are in your hands. The knowledge is in your mind. The opportunity is in front of you.

Now it is time to move forward.

How to Get a Personalized SBA Commercial Mortgage Review

If you found this book helpful, you may want to see how these strategies apply to your specific financial situation.

SBA commercial mortgage financing is highly customized—your business income, financial statements, credit profile, property type, industry, and long-term goals all play a role in determining what you qualify for and how your loan should be structured.

Every borrower's situation is different. Your revenue trends, business model, tax returns, debt obligations, ownership structure, and the type of commercial property you are purchasing, refinancing, or building all impact your options. The strategies and examples in this book are designed to teach you how SBA commercial mortgage loans work—but your actual loan approval, terms, and structure can only be determined by analyzing your real financial profile.

If you would like a no-obligation SBA Commercial Mortgage review, you can request one here:

Email: info@FinibiMortgage.com

A licensed mortgage broker will review your business financials, income structure, credit profile, and goals, and explain what SBA financing options may be available to you—including:

• SBA 7(a) commercial mortgage loans• SBA 504 fixed-rate commercial real estate financing• Owner-occupied property qualification strategies• Business acquisition with real estate financing• Commercial refinance and cash-out strategies• Construction and expansion loan structuring• Advanced SBA deal structuring to maximize approval

No cost. No pressure. No obligation.

Sincerely,

Joseph G. Correa

Finibi Mortgage Inc.

Licensed Mortgage Broker

About the Author

Joseph G. Correa is a licensed mortgage broker and the founder of Finibi Mortgage, a Florida-based brokerage specializing in SBA commercial mortgage loans, non-QM lending, and strategic real estate financing solutions for business owners, entrepreneurs, and investors.

With more than two decades of experience in mortgage lending, underwriting, and deal structuring, Joseph has helped thousands of clients secure financing for commercial real estate, business acquisitions, and complex transactions using both traditional and alternative lending strategies.

Unlike traditional loan officers who focus only on basic qualification, Joseph's approach emphasizes **cash flow analysis, deal structuring, and strategic financing**. He believes that business owners should not be limited by rigid lending formulas, but instead empowered by understanding how to structure deals that align with lender guidelines and maximize approval potential.

Joseph is widely recognized for his expertise in:

• SBA 7(a) and SBA 504 commercial mortgage loans• Owner-occupied commercial real estate financing• Business acquisition with real estate structuring• Commercial refinance and cash flow optimization• Construction and expansion financing• Advanced loan structuring and approval strategy

Through his education platform, Finibi Academy, Joseph has trained tens of thousands of students worldwide in mortgage strategy, real estate investing, credit optimization, and financial independence.

He created the *SBA Commercial Mortgage Loan Mastery Series* to provide a clear, step-by-step roadmap for borrowers and professionals who want to understand, qualify for, and scale commercial real estate using SBA financing.

His mission is simple:

To help business owners use strategic financing to acquire assets, build cash flow, and create long-term wealth.

When he is not structuring loans or writing, Joseph works with clients across the United States to design customized SBA financing strategies aligned with their business goals and growth plans.

The SBA Commercial Mortgage Loan Mastery Series Roadmap

The Complete Guide to Using SBA Financing to Build Commercial Real Estate and Business Wealth

The purpose of *The SBA Commercial Mortgage Loan Mastery Series* is to give business owners, investors, and mortgage professionals the exact strategies used by lenders and underwriters—translated into simple, practical steps you can apply in real life.

This series takes you from beginner to advanced mastery of how to qualify, structure, and scale commercial real estate and business financing using SBA mortgage loans.

Each book builds on the last. You are not just learning how to get approved—you are learning how to control your approvals and scale your opportunities.

Book 1 — SBA Commercial Mortgage Loan Fundamentals Understand how SBA mortgage programs work, including 7(a) and 504 loans, and how to qualify.

Book 2 — Getting Approved for an SBA Commercial Mortgage Loan Learn step-by-step strategies to meet lender requirements and secure funding.

Book 3 — Owner-Occupied Property Financing with SBA Loans Learn how to buy or refinance your business property using SBA financing.

Book 4 — Buying a Business and Real Estate with SBA Financing Acquire a business and its property in one structured transaction.

Book 5 — SBA 7(a) Mortgage Loan Strategies Master flexible loan structures for business and real estate funding.

Book 6 — SBA 504 Mortgage Loans for Commercial Real Estate Use long-term fixed-rate financing for large property acquisitions.

Book 7 — Refinancing Commercial Debt with SBA Loans Lower payments, improve cash flow, and restructure existing debt.

Book 8 — SBA Loans for Construction and Expansion Build, renovate, and scale commercial properties with structured financing.

Book 9 — SBA Loan Requirements, Rates, and Structures Understand how to compare options and choose the best loan.

Book 10 — Advanced SBA Commercial Mortgage Structuring Engineer approvals and maximize leverage using expert strategies.

This series is designed to move you from:

Understanding → Execution → Scaling → Mastery

By the end, you will not just know how to qualify—you will know how to structure, analyze, and scale deals like a professional.

Educational & Financial Disclaimer

The *SBA Commercial Mortgage Loan Mastery Series* is intended for educational and informational purposes only.

This content is designed to help readers understand SBA commercial mortgage lending, real estate financing strategies, and business acquisition concepts. It is not financial, legal, tax, or investment advice.

Joseph G. Correa and Live Stronger Faster are not acting as your personal financial advisor, attorney, accountant, or mortgage professional through this publication.

SBA loan programs, underwriting guidelines, interest rates, and lender requirements may change at any time and vary by lender.

All examples in this series are for illustration purposes only and do not guarantee approval or results.

Always consult with licensed professionals before making financial decisions.

Risk Disclosure

SBA commercial mortgage lending and real estate investing involve risk.

Business performance, income stability, interest rate changes, market conditions, and lender guidelines can all impact loan approval and financial outcomes.

Borrowing against real estate or using leverage increases both potential returns and risk.

Failure to repay a loan may result in foreclosure and loss of property.

Cash flow, rental income, appreciation, and business performance are not guaranteed.

All strategies presented in this series are educational and must be evaluated based on your individual financial situation.

You are solely responsible for your financial decisions.

www.ingramcontent.com/pod-product-compliance
Ingram Content Group UK Ltd.
Pitfield, Milton Keynes, MK11 3LW, UK
UKHW020159290926
15471UKWH00005B/953

9 798295 820663